W9-AJR-433

B A L T I M O R E
A PORTRAIT

Ron Pilling
Chris Bohaska
Writers

Roger Miller
Photographer

Photo of Roger Miller

IMAGE PUBLISHING, LTD.

IMAGE PUBLISHING, LTD.
1411 Hollins Street/Union Square
410-566-1222   Baltimore, Maryland 21223   FAX 410-233-1241

DEDICATION

RUTH DORA MILLER AND **CHARLES JOHN EDWARD MILLER**
I would like to dedicate this book to my parents for their love, friendship and patience. Thank you!

Roger Miller, 8-8-83

How can two people keep getting better?

Roger Miller, 7-7-88

I would like to re-dedicate this new book to my parents, **Ruth Dora Miller** and **Charles John Edward Miller** for their enduring spirit and almost unwavering belief in my photography and my books. Thank you for your continuous patience, friendship and love.

Roger Miller, 8-8-93

SPECIAL THANKS

I would like to thank everyone who had a part in this project. I would especially like to thank the following:

A special thanks to all the people and businesses of Baltimore and Maryland. Without their hard work and dedication to making our city and Maryland the great state it is, this book would not have been possible.

I would like to thank **Mayor Kurt L. Schmoke** for his assistance in writing the foreword to "Baltimore A Portrait."

A very special thanks to **Wayne Chapell**, Executive Director of the Baltimore Area Convention and Visitors Association, for his friendship, foresight and commitment to new ideas to promote both Baltimore and Maryland.

I would like to thank **Charlene Allison Briggs** for dealing with the pressures we have had to finish this book.

A very special thanks to **Tom Carter** of Old Bay Financial for his assistance, friendship, advice, and action.

A very special thanks to **Lynn Moquin, CPA** for her financial advice, friendship and moral support over the last couple of years.

I would like to thank **The Bank of Glen Burnie** for their belief in my work and the opportunity to continue to create our books.

Roger Miller, 8-8-93

CREDITS

Photography by Roger Miller
Design by David Miller
Text by Ron Pilling
Text for Sports & Recreation and captions by Christopher Bohaska
Typesetting and layouts by Delta Graphics & Communications, Inc.
Color separations in Hong Kong by Oriental Graphics, Inc.
Printed in Hong Kong.

INFORMATION

All rights reserved. No part of this book may be reproduced or transmitted in any form or by any means, electronic or mechanical, including photocopying or recording, or by any information storage and retrieval system, without permission in writing from the publisher.

©-1993 by Image Publishing, LTD. Compilation and writing, all rights reserved - 3rd Edition.
©-1993 by Roger Miller, Photographer. Photography, all rights reserved - 3rd Edition.

ISBN #: 0-911897-23-2 (3rd Edition)
ISBN #: 0-911897-14-3 (2nd Edition Hardcover)
ISBN #: 0-911897-15-1 (2nd Edition Softcover)
ISBN #: 0-911897-00-3 (1st Edition Hardcover)
ISBN #: 0-911897-01-1 (1st Edition Softcover)

Library of Congress Catalog Card Number:
1993 3rd Edition Hardcover: 93-061093
1988 2nd Edition Hardcover: 88-081951
1988 2nd Edition Softcover: 88-081951
1983 1st Edition Hardcover: 82-091142
1983 1st Edition Softcover: 83-090131

First Printing, First Edition 1983; Second Printing, First Edition 1984; Third Printing, First Edition 1985; Fourth Printing Second Edition 1988; Fifth printing, Second Edition 1990; Sixth printing, Third Edition 1993.

ORDERS

For direct orders please call or write for specific cost and postage and handling to the above address. Discounts available for stores, institutions and corporations, minimum orders required.

Baltimore's dramatic skyline rises from the Inner Harbor, the heart and soul of the city.
Seemingly timeless yet ever-changing, the face of the city has evolved over the past few decades,
creating one of the world's most impressive and innovative ports. Nestled in this architectural gem
are attractions stretching from and including the Pier Six Pavilion, the National Aquarium,
Harborplace, and finally the new home of the Orioles at Camden Yards.

Late into the night, lights from all over the city show visitors the way to endless discoveries and delights.
Whether it's a quiet water taxi ride on the harbor's calm waters, sampling Maryland seafood in a local
waterside restaurant, or taking in a concert with friends on a warm summer night,
the city stays up late to offer a cornucopia of pleasures for all the senses.

TABLE OF CONTENTS

Baltimore City Hall

Kurt L. Schmoke, Mayor

Kurt L. Schmoke, Mayor

Originally built in 1875, Baltimore's City Hall was designed by a young architect, George Frederick.
It is an early example of French Renaissance architecture in the U.S. A national historic landmark structure,
City Hall was built almost entirely by local craftsmen with local materials. It survived
the Great Fire of 1904, but succumbed to gradual deterioration until the citizens of Baltimore
decided to renovate the once majestic building. Completed in 1977,
the restoration gracefully integrated past and present.

FOREWORD

By Kurt L. Schmoke, Mayor

One of the most common reactions of first-time visitors to Baltimore is,"This is Baltimore?"

Yes, this is Baltimore.

For the people and families who have grown up in Baltimore (many of whom trace their Baltimore roots back for generations), and for the newly arrived as well, Baltimore is a treasure filled city, rich in history, architecture, music, food, waterfront beauty, literature, science and identity.

It's this last quality - identity - that makes Baltimore particularly special. Baltimore is a city with character. It is the home or birthplace of Justice Thurgood Marshall, Anne Tyler, Eubie Blake and Barry Levinson, among other distinguished Americans. Baltimore's cultural, linguistic and historical flavor sets it apart, and makes it a place you want to come home to.

The people of Baltimore are tremendously proud of the changes that have taken place here in the last 15 years - many of which are showcased in this book. But even without the Inner Harbor, the Gallery and the other gleaming new office buildings, Baltimore would still be the place we would want to raise our children. That is because beyond the Harbor, the Washington Monument and the homes of H.L. Mencken, Babe Ruth, and Edgar Allan Poe, are the homes and neighborhoods of the people of Baltimore. And it's there that Baltimore's identity comes to life.

Whether you visit Hampstead Hill in East Baltimore, Union Square in West Baltimore, Roland Park, Federal Hill, Windsor Hills, Charles Village, Highlandtown, Forest Park or any of Baltimore's other proud neighborhoods, you will find the beauty and energy of Baltimore. Each of these communities has a color, shape and texture all its own, and together they give Baltimore its special signature - as a place where families can grow and prosper, and business and visitors are always welcome.

Making Baltimore a national attraction - which resulted from the public and private sectors working together - has stimulated neighborhood preservation and revitalization efforts. These efforts are being led by partnerships composed of business, community and religious organizations, and government. Homes are being restored, and whole neighborhoods - including commercial districts - are being rebuilt.

Also located in Baltimore are internationally renowned hospitals, museums, universities, and industrial research centers. Scholarship, creativity and scientific discovery have long flourished in Baltimore and will continue to do so.

There is a consensus in Baltimore that this city - which at one time had been nearly written off as an example of industrial and urban decay - should serve as a model for what can be accomplished by any proud and hardworking community.

Baltimore always had hope and promise, and now we have much to show for it. Since the first edition of Roger Miller's "Baltimore A Portrait," the Baltimore skyline has changed significantly. The Walters Art Gallery has been renovated, an IMAX theater has been added to the Maryland Science Center. Old factories have been converted into comfortable downtown living spaces for thousands of people, and modern movie and entertainment complexes have been built or are under construction.

As for the future, the Columbus Center will be added to the Inner Harbor, the Convention Center will be expanded, and if awarded the NFL franchise, Baltimore will be rewarded with a football stadium to be built in Camden Yards. And that is only the beginning. With their creative drive and cooperative spirit, the people of Baltimore will continue to remake this city without ever relinquishing its historic character.

I invite you to look through the pages of this book. Go slowly and enjoy the view. Baltimore is a wonderful blend of old and new, and Roger Miller has beautifully captured the essence of both.

Baltimore, you will quickly discover, is a wonderful place to live.

Kurt L. Schmoke, Mayor

The sun sets on a vista of Baltimore which didn't exist just a few short years ago.
This view from a high-rise in the Canton area, east of Fells Point, was not very long ago
deteriorated docks and shutdown manufacturing plants. Today Canton consists more of
up-scale town houses, high-rises, and modern marinas.

HISTORY

On a warm spring morning a soldier leans against a high wooden piling, watching out across the Baltimore harbor through a forest of tall masts, a web of tarred rigging. He wears the uniform of a foot soldier of the First Maryland Regiment, indirectly under the command of General George Washington. His musket leans against one leg, his leather haversack hangs loosely from the post.

But wait, this is not Revolutionary War Baltimore. It is the twentieth century, and the infantryman will be marching in a parade from East Baltimore's Fells Point to Federal Hill, overlooking the Inner Harbor. The event commemorates the 200th anniversary of the signing of the Constitution by the State of Maryland. Like the celebration of two centuries earlier, Baltimoreans portraying the trades of the waning 1700's - shipwrights, blacksmiths, apothecaries and more - will parade through Baltimore streets praising the document wrought by Marylanders and others in Philadelphia. The only difference is that these modern Baltimoreans merely dress the part.

For this is Baltimore, Maryland, a city proud of its three hundred years of progress but a city which, fortunately, refuses to let go of the past.

When the returning soldiers from the Revolutionary War laid aside their weapons and went back to the shipyards, the brickworks, the breweries and the docks along the city's Patapsco River, they were unknowingly laying the foundations for a city which, by the time of the Constitutional Bicentennial, would be the focal point for over a million Marylanders. Baltimore has become the region's banking and financial headquarters, a major center of manufacturing, and a cornerstone in the transportation industry of the entire East Coast.

It all began at this spot where the accountant, costumed as an eighteenth century soldier, scans the modern Inner Harbor. The earliest known picture of the city, depicting Baltimore in 1752, shows a small but thriving town. A cluster of a dozen or so buildings; simple box-like houses, a tavern or two, a church and several small businesses dot the hillside overlooking the harbor. Baltimore Town was dwarfed by Jonestown and Fells Point to the east, both major centers of trade and shipbuilding. The three would become the nucleus of the modern city of Baltimore.

By the Revolutionary War there were nearly six hundred houses dominating the harborscape. Economic growth, especially along the creek valleys to the north, was creating a class of landed gentry and merchants that had a decided stake in the trading interests that operated along the narrow alleys and wooden wharves of the Patapsco Basin. Two commodities - iron and wheat - drove the local economy during its important early years. The streams that ran into Baltimore from the hills to the north and west provided power for the water-driven mills that threshed the grain and hammered the iron bars that eventually made their way to the harbor. Many early attempts to establish towns in the Chesapeake Bay watershed had failed, but Baltimore, with its natural harbor, its rich resources and its proximity to the productive lands nearby, became the state's major market center by the close of the Revolution.

In 1776, John Adams visited Baltimore while serving in the Continental Congress. Its merchants were prosperous and its businesses flourishing, and the Massachusetts congressman admired the revolutionary spirit of the people. Perhaps it was our war for independence that set Baltimore squarely on the road to greatness. The war generated tremendous demand for the town's two most important products, iron and wheat, allowing Baltimore families to participate actively in the struggle for freedom from England. Being a shipbuilding center, Baltimore contributed 250 privateers (little more than pirates, but the nucleus of the fledgling American Navy) to the fight. The growth of manufacturing helped the city break from the tobacco-farming tradition. The city opened its arms to immigrants from Ireland and Germany, Scotland and France, and each new group contributed to Baltimore's rapid expansion.

By the time Jonestown, Fells Point, and Baltimore Town were incorporated into one city, the economic direction had long been decided. There was much rivalry between the three villages that coalesced into a mercantile power, differences that mark the city and give it much of its character to this day. In 1796, when Baltimore was officially incorporated, the residents thought of their home not as a village, but as a city, and Baltimore had become an important cog in the financial and trade machinery of the western world.

A post-Revolution generation took the reins of progress and the city entered a period of rapid expansion that would continue unabated in spite of the British bombardment of Baltimore's Fort McHenry in 1814. Financial institutions were created to meet the tremendous demand for banking and brokerage services. A host of related trades sprang up in the closing years of the 1700's. There were six newspapers on the streets by 1799, the number of printers and publishers quadrupled, and an entire community of craftsmen - shipfitters, brewers, bakers, soap boilers, leatherworkers, and coopers - sprang up as a direct result of commercial growth.

So it was that Baltimore found herself in an enviable position when the War of 1812 broke out. She sent hundreds of privateers in the feared "Baltimore Clippers," low-slung sailboats built for speed as well as for cargo, against the powerful British fleet. In September, 1814, British forces under General Robert Ross sailed up the Chesapeake to crush the "nest of pirates." Meeting defeat at the hands of the Baltimore militia near North Point, and repulsed after a 24-hour bombardment of Fort McHenry at the mouth of the harbor, the invaders sailed away.

It was during the bombardment that Francis Scott Key, a local lawyer who observed the merciless cannonading from the decks of a British frigate, was inspired to pen what would become the National Anthem. Within days the poem became a rallying cry, and Baltimoreans were overnight heroes.

Within three months the war was over and Baltimore could return its attention to economic growth. Peace brought prosperity, the clipper ships returned to trade, and steam power carried the city into a new industrial era. In the first forty years of the 1800's the population expanded from about twenty-five thousand to over a hundred thousand. New roads connected Baltimore with cities to the west, canals were built to move goods to the growing region along the Ohio River, and the railroad was born. In 1830, the Baltimore and Ohio Railroad started the first commercial rail service in the country, and Baltimore became the first city of rail travel. Dominance in railroading would sustain the unheralded growth for over seventy years.

It was the city's fortunate location which fostered this expansion. Baltimore was the closest port city to Pittsburgh, cutting out over a hundred miles of land transportation compared to either Philadelphia or Alexandria. The birth of the railroad here strengthened Baltimore's commercial dominance and spurred the city's continued growth.

Viewed from the air, or from the water's edge, the multitude of architectural styles symbolically reflect the diversity and integration of Baltimore's many nationalities and neighborhoods. With contemporary shopping areas, modern skyscrapers and historic rowhouses all sharing common space, the city reveals itself as a place with a vision toward the future while remaining proud of its historic past.
This, above all else, may be Baltimore's most precious heritage.

On the eve of the Civil War, Baltimore found itself a city divided. Though most of its trade was with the North, there was a strong attachment to the Confederate states. Landed gentry whose plantations surrounded Baltimore still owned slaves. While some Baltimoreans supported Lincoln in the election of 1861, others openly espoused secession. On April 19 the first blood of the war was shed on Baltimore streets when troops of the Sixth Massachusetts Regiment were attacked by a Baltimore mob. Throughout the rest of the war the city was virtually captive, guarded by 1500 federal troops armed with heavy cannon commanding a threatening position from Federal Hill.

The city remained relatively unscathed during the war and emerged to continue its earlier mercantile domination of the Mid-Atlantic region. The decades between the Civil War and World War I saw both economic and social change. Horse car lines, and later trolleys, enabled Baltimoreans to move away from the harbor. Public education offered new opportunities to a generation of Baltimoreans, and men who had made huge fortunes here gave some of their wealth back to a grateful population.

In 1866, philanthropist George Peabody dedicated the Peabody Institute, a world-respected center of musical education. Enoch Pratt's generous donation to the city of Baltimore resulted in the opening of the Enoch Pratt Library in 1886. Johns Hopkins gave much of his multi-million dollar estate for the creation of Johns Hopkins Hospital and University. Merchant Moses Sheppard created what would become the Sheppard and Enoch Pratt Hospital. Dozens of other moneyed Baltimoreans did the same, founding schools, hospitals, and museums. After a century of continual growth, Baltimore was beginning to become a well-rounded city, offering opportunities that would enrich the lives of many of its residents.

The period between the Civil War and World War I saw the greatest influx of immigrants to Baltimore in its entire history. Most came from Germany and Ireland, though Czechs, Poles, Jews, Lithuanians and others from Eastern Europe also passed through the Locust Point reception center. Ethnic neighborhoods, like Little Italy just east of the Inner Harbor, the Greek neighborhood along Eastern Avenue, Little Lithuania scattered around Lithuanian Hall on Hollins Street, and the Polish enclave in Fells Point near St. Stanislaus Church, remain as testament to the courage and industry of the new Americans.

While people were on their way to church on February 7, 1904, an event which would both mark the opening of the new century and contribute to changing the face of the city for decades was smoldering in the dry goods warehouse of the John F. Hurst Company on Hopkins Place. The Great Baltimore Fire destroyed over a thousand commercial buildings and scorched one hundred and forty acres. By the time the flames reached Jones Falls early Monday morning, fire companies from as far away as Philadelphia had rushed to the scene by special train to assist the Baltimore firefighters.

The city quickly went on to rebuild. The financial center, where most of the damage had occurred, moved ahead with scarcely a pause. Though many local insurance companies were bankrupted by ensuing claims, the fire represented little more than a pause in Baltimore's economic progress.

Baltimoreans contributed to the war efforts in both World Wars by sending their sons to fight and by redoubling manufacturing efforts to meet the nation's requirements for armaments. Seemingly Baltimore was destined to move into the second half of the twentieth century with its historic, economic and social power intact.

But like all older, manufacturing-based American cities, Baltimore was to experience both economic and social change beyond anything in her three hundred year history. By 1950 a third of the population lived in poverty and local leadership had to face the problems. Black leaders began to move into elective offices in Baltimore much earlier than in any other southern city, contributing to the city's relatively early advances toward racial and social equality.

In 1961, the groundbreaking for One Charles Center marked the beginning of a major downtown renewal effort that shifted into high gear in the 1970's and 1980's. An unheralded partnership between local government and private investment began to change the face of the city.

The election of William Donald Schaefer to the mayoralty in 1971 added a powerful catalyst to the process. Schaefer, a combination of unabashed cheerleader for the city, determined negotiator, deal maker, and publicist extraordinaire, had a vision for Baltimore that to most seemed impossibly progressive. Even Baltimoreans themselves, especially those who had fled the city for the suburbs during the fifties and sixties, thought that Schaefer was a dreamer.

That he was, but his dreams quickly became true. He saw in Baltimore a city whose unique character could attract millions of visitors each year, visitors who would spend their money along the harbor's edge and in doing so create jobs and prosperity. When Harborplace opened in 1980 no one could argue about the Mayor's success or about the new face of a town that newspapers across the country had begun to call "Charm City."

As energetic new city homeowners begin to restore the ancient brick rowhouses that line Baltimore streets, entire neighborhoods take on a new pride and a new charisma. It seems that a new restaurant opens in Baltimore every week or so and major hotel chains fight for land near the Inner Harbor. Conventioneers book city facilities years in advance. With a new respect for itself, Baltimore is looking forward to the twenty-first century, confident that the enthusiasm and industry of her residents will assure her continued growth.

Once a major port for commercial shipping, the Inner Harbor has developed into one of the prime areas
for pleasure boating up and down the Eastern Seaboard. Boaters from nearby Annapolis, as well
as sailors from around the world, have sailed into the still waters of the harbor. Boats used for
entertaining, for taxi services, and for educational purposes all return home to the harbor
from trips up and down the Chesapeake Bay.

INNER HARBOR

If ever a city could boast that in returning to its roots it found the resources it needed to face an uncertain future, Baltimore is that city. For in Baltimore, the focus of the city fathers has returned time and time again to the harbor. The most recent return, however - the one that capitalized the words "Inner Harbor" - marked both a dramatic change in the traditional role of the waterfront in Baltimore, as well as a direction for the city for decades to come.

Baltimore's Inner Harbor is the jewel in the crown of the city's renaissance. Its success is symbolic of the vision of a handful of business and government leaders who saw in their hometown more than just a blue-collar working city. The millions who visit the Inner Harbor each year attest to the wisdom of that vision, and the harbor's pavilions, shops and restaurants are usually the first stops for out-of-towners.

Years after its opening, the National Aquarium still draws huge crowds that line up daily outside the glass pavilion on Pier 3. A stop for lunch at Harborplace, perhaps a crab cake or half-a-dozen Chincoteague oysters, is a must on the day's schedule. There's exclusive shopping at The Gallery, paddle-boats, the spectacular IMAX movie theatre in the Maryland Science Center and dozens of other attractions in the panorama tightly woven around the Patapsco Basin.

Yet just thirty years ago the harbor was the last place a native would want to take his uncle and aunt from Tulsa for a day's enjoyment. Rotting piers lined the Light Street side of the harbor. There was little commercial shipping, though the odd, rust-streaked tramp freighter would pull up from time to time. If there was any nighttime action at all, it was probably at the City Morgue, just a block or two from the present Harborplace.

This is the same harbor which, in the 1752 drawing of Baltimore Town, was a pastoral village. Several fishermen pull their nets in the shadow of Federal Hill while a single sloop rides at anchor on what would become the Light Street bulkhead. A couple dozen buildings rise on the gentle slope, and plowed fields cover the site of today's Pier 6 Harborlights Pavilion.

It was the protected Patapsco Basin which drew people here in the first place, and the basin would be the focal point of the town well into the twentieth century. Early photographs show an observation tower atop Federal Hill, whose red clay flanks drop precipitously to the water. Tall-masted boats line all three banks. The wharves along Light and Pratt Streets teem with horse-drawn wagons filled with all imaginable cargoes. The lines of wagons often extended for blocks in every direction.

Along Light Street stood the offices and wharves of companies that offered steamboat service for both passengers and cargo up and down the Chesapeake. Their destinations - Richmond, Petersburg, Raleigh and Lynchburg - were painted in gilt letters along their bracketed rooflines. Women with parasols and men in stovepipe hats fought their way past the drovers to claim a berth.

After over two centuries of productive commercial activities, the basin in the 1950's had sunk to its lowest level. Shipping had moved to the outer harbor and the buildings that surrounded the Basin were abandoned, crumbling. What had been the city's gate to the world was an embarrassing eyesore.

Under the leadership of Mayor William Donald Schaefer, however, the focus of city development looked once again to the Inner Harbor. The mayor proposed a broad, energetic development plan that would make the old Basin the centerpiece of the new Baltimore. In a new spirit of cooperation, government learned to work with developers whose contributions could match the mayor's vision. By September 1979, when ground was broken for Harborplace, that dream was well on its way to reality.

Developer James Rouse's Harborplace pavilions have become the anchor in an exciting panorama of new buildings, or new uses for old buildings. One of the green-roofed Harborplace buildings houses shops and restaurants, and the other is a festival of small food vendors, restaurants and tiny shops. Chesapeake Bay fare - crabs, clams, corn-on-the-cob, fish and fried chicken - are staples here, complemented by a mouth-watering vista of international foods. Shops feature everything from local crafts and souvenirs to high fashion.

Anchored in the shelter of Harborplace is the U.S.F. Constellation, the first ship launched by the United States Navy in 1797, built in nearby Harris Creek just a mile or so from its present berth. The Constellation has been recently restored and dramatizes shipboard life from the early days of the country.

The Constellation is the focal point for a growing regatta of historic boats and ships as well as private pleasure craft. During summer months, the Chesapeake Bay Skipjack Minnie V sails daily from the Inner Harbor for waterfront tours (in the winter she still dredges for oysters). The Lady Maryland, a reproduction Pungy Schooner, provides a classroom-on-the-water for Baltimore schoolchildren.

Baltimore's "floating ambassador," the Pride of Baltimore II, also calls the Inner Harbor its home port. The Pride II, begun in 1987 after a tragic storm took her namesake, will sail around the globe spreading the good news about Baltimore. A reproduction of the famous Baltimore Clippers, the Pride II is low and fast; beautiful under sail.

Among the first new buildings on the Inner Harbor was the Maryland Science Center, home of the Maryland Academy of Sciences, the oldest scientific academy in the nation. This contemporary building at the harbor's southwest corner houses the Davis Planetarium, and displays everything from computers to Chesapeake Bay ecology. Its newest addition is the IMAX movie theatre featuring a tall, wrap-around screen that truly brings its presentations into three-dimensional life.

The harbor's most popular attraction has always been the National Aquarium. A dynamic building, with a rain forest housed in a glass pyramid which overlooks the Constellation's berth, the aquarium is home to 6000 specimens - fish, reptiles, tropical plants, and more. Animals and plants are displayed in life-like artificial environments, including the tropical rain forest, a shark tank, and an Atlantic coral reef.

So in just several decades, the Basin has become the Inner Harbor. There is more, like the Top of the World, an observation deck atop the World Trade Center featuring displays of harbor history, the Pier 6 concert pavilion, and The Gallery, a sparkling new multi-level shopping mall attached to Stouffer Harborplace Hotel. Baltimoreans and out-of-town guests alike flock to the new Inner Harbor, just as Baltimoreans have returned to the harbor year after year, century after century.

Many people say the early evening hours in summer are the best time to visit Harborplace.
When buildings cast long, moody shadows from the setting sun, and cool breezes rush up
from off of the water, the tempo here slows to a leisurely pace and the Southern charm
of the city reveals itself. Joggers and walkers alike venture around the wide sidewalks from
Pier Six to Federal Hill,

The Inner Harbor area offers a wide array of eating and shopping experiences.
Harborplace, which includes both the Light Street and Pratt Street Pavilions, contains
a variety of shops and restaurants that are bound to satisfy any taste or whim.
The Gallery, a block north of Harborplace, is a suburban-type mall in a city setting
that is packed with fine shops and eateries. Unique shops, restaurants and galleries also line
the streets north of the harbor, inviting the curious and the adventurous to explore further into the city
for exciting, undiscovered treasures and foods.

For those wanting to forego the shopping experience, there are still plenty of things to do and see at Harborplace. Water taxis make frequent trips to and from historic Fells Point, where many clubs and restaurants await. Fireworks at the harbor on Independence Day have become a yearly ritual that attract huge summer crowds. Ship enthusiasts can visit the Constellation or any of the ships from faraway lands that dock here on a regular basis. And musicians, magicians and street performers regularly perform to enthusiastic audiences on the wide sidewalks at the juncture of the Pavilions.

One of the most overlooked, but most exciting, treats at Harborplace are the crowds. People of all ages and places line the walks as far as the eye can see, making people-watching one of the most interesting by-products of a visit to the Inner Harbor. Festivals, foreign ships and just plain great weather bring the crowds out, and sometimes it seems as if everyone in the city is here to see or meet someone.

The Clipper City is just one of the many boats that are available for cruises through the harbor
and on the Chesapeake Bay. The ship has been hired for parties, cruises and more than a few weddings.
Over the years, it has become part of the Inner Harbor landscape. It is a ship that is both beautiful
to look at and exiting on which to travel.

The Gallery, a multi-story shopping mall that is connected to the Stouffer Hotel, is jam-packed with fine shops, eateries and galleries around a garden-like plaza. Situated across Pratt Street from Harborplace, its dining areas offer wonderful views of the harbor, as well as some of the best sight-lines in the city for parades that pass by down Pratt Street. Skywalks connect The Gallery with the Pratt Street Pavilion in Harborplace, making access easy and safe.

One of the most eye-catching structures on the harbor is the National Aquarium. Located on Pier Three, just a block from Harborplace, the Aquarium houses a huge variety of fish, birds and mammals in a setting that is up-close and strikingly realistic. Exhibits are educational and breathtaking, and a wide range of environments are created, including a famous rain forest that tops the building. Recently, a new mammal pavilion was added, where dolphin shows have received rave reviews from visitors.

Since it first opened its doors, the National Aquarium has attracted long lines on Pier Three.
And it's no wonder. The Aquarium's educational displays on marine life are perfect
for school field trips. Most of all though, the crowds wait in line for a look at over 6,000 specimens,
all in brilliantly constructed environments that include fish, mammals, tropical plants and reptilian life.
Visitors practically walk right through the striking environments, enabling them to be surrounded
by the marine life that is on display here.

21

The newest extension on the National Aquarium is the Mammal Pavilion, which is devoted
to the study and display of such water mammals as dolphins, whales and porpoises.
The Aquarium allows such marine life to be studied by some of the world's leading scientists.
Popular dolphin shows have attracted enthusiastic crowds of all ages, making the National Aquarium
one of Baltimore's most visited, and beloved, attractions.

The display of trained dolphins at the National Aquarium has become one of the most popular attractions
on the harbor in Baltimore. These playful and intelligent animals delight crowds of all ages
at the Mammal Pavilion, which is one of the newest additions to the Inner Harbor landscape.

U.S.F. Constellation

U.S.F. Constellation

U.S.F. Constellation

Launched by the U.S. Navy in 1797, the U.S.F. Constellation is the centerpiece of Baltimore's contribution
to the nation's naval history. Located at the juncture of the Harborplace Pavilions, the warship is
just one of many historic boats and ships that rest in the docks of the harbor. Recently restored
to its original splendor, visitors on board will appreciate what the sailing life was like on a battleship
dating from the early days of our history.

Schooner races

Visit of Columbus' Ships

Visit of Columbus' Ships

Many historic and beautiful ships from all over the world visit Baltimore's Inner Harbor.
The display of tall ships during the country's Bicentennial celebration is still talked about by locals
who remember that dramatic water parade. Recently, replicas of Columbus' three famous ships -
the Nina, the Pinta and the Santa Maria - were on hand for the 500th anniversary of America's discovery.
All during the year, ships of all types and sizes are on view in the harbor at Harborplace.

Serving as Baltimore's floating ambassador around the world, the Pride of Baltimore II is a beautiful replica
of Baltimore's famous clipper ships. Begun in 1987, after the original Pride was lost in a storm at sea,
the Pride II has become an important link between the city's past and its future.

Styled after early naval ships that were built in Baltimore, the Pride of Baltimore II is a combination of old and new in Baltimore's sailing history. Typical of the ships built between the nation's two wars with England in the late 18th and early 19th centuries, the Pride II sports state-of-the-art equipment and designs that make it sleek and fast as it sails down the Chesapeake Bay and around the world.

The Pier Six Pavilion, located several blocks east of Harborplace, is a wonderful place to catch a concert on a warm summer night. Music enthusiasts, who hear great music emanating from the futuristic, tent-like designed structure, are lured from all around the harbor. Cool breezes and the quiet sounds of the harbor blend beautifully with the traditional fare of classical, folk and jazz music, making for a truly unique and delightful Baltimore experience.

Viewed from the air, the expansion of the Inner Harbor area certainly must include
Baltimore's newest gem, Oriole Park at Camden Yards. Completed for the opening of the
1992 Major League season, the new home of the Orioles has received international acclaim
for its design, which combines the best elements of historic ballparks with modern day conveniences.
One of its most distinct features is the Camden Yards warehouse, which stretches
from the parking lot to the right field bleachers.

With offices located in a restored lighthouse at the Inner Harbor, The Living Classrooms Foundation is
an organization devoted to working with inner city youth. Founded in 1985,
the Foundation provides young people with hands-on instruction that will help them
develop skills relating to boat carpentry, motor repair and boat handling. Sailing trips on the bay,
and camping adventures at the Foundation's llama farm in Harford County, also instill
personal confidence and teamwork skills for underprivileged children yearning to improve their lives.

The Lady Maryland, the centerpiece of the Living Classrooms Foundation, is just one of many boats
either built or restored by special students at the Foundation's Maritime Institute.
The ship is available for group trips and school studies of and on the Chesapeake Bay.
Through the Foundation, students learn more about the bay and its environment, as well as develop skills
to better prepare themselves for entry level jobs in marine trades, a growing industry in the Baltimore area.

Looking down and across the harbor from Federal Hill, the city's lights reflect the pride of its residents
and businesses alike. Lights marking all kinds of special occasions – in this case, Baltimore's hosting of
Major League Baseball's All-Star game – shimmer off the glassy water of the harbor. The city also shows off
its lights during other notable yearly occasions, especially Christmas and Independence Day.
Fourth of July fireworks are particularly dramatic from this late-evening perch on Federal Hill.

The Davis Planetarium

The Maryland Science Center

The Maryland Science Center, IMAX on right

Located in Harborplace, the Maryland Science Center is the home of the Maryland Academy of Sciences, the oldest organization in the country devoted to the study of science. Displays at the Science Center, which include exhibits on electricity, optics and the environment, will fascinate visitors of all ages. The Davis Planetarium is a stargazer's delight, with a stunning program that maps the planets and stars of the universe. The IMAX Theatre, one of afew in the world, is a breathtaking movie theatre that features specially filmed movies on a huge wrap-around screen.

33

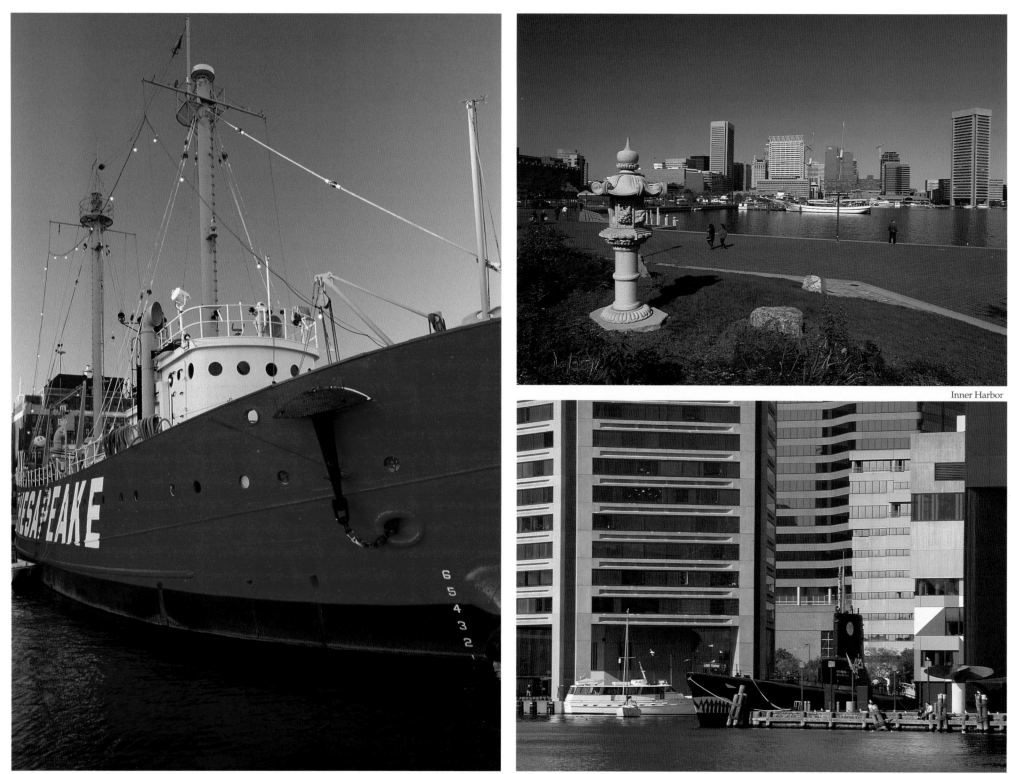

Light Ship Chesapeake

Inner Harbor

U.S.S. Torsk

Capturing the spirit of Baltimore's seafaring heritage, several historic ships at the Inner Harbor
share space with the pleasure boats that anchor nearby. Along with the U.S.F. Constellation,
the harbor is home to the Chesapeake, Coast Guard ships, and the U.S.S. Torsk,
a unique World War II submarine which is open to the public. All of these ships at the harbor
help capture Baltimore's spirit, and her continuing love affair with the open sea.

Marina, Inner Harbor

U.S. Coast Guard Cutter Taney

World Trade Center

From a foot bridge across a pier, or from just about any angle, the World Trade Center is one of many focal points that rises from the harbor's edge. Designed by world-famous architect I.M. Pei, this informal headquarters of international trade and shipping in the Mid-Atlantic was begun in 1968, and was one of the first structures built during the Inner Harbor's renaissance. The "Top of the World," an observation room atop the Center, provides a spectacular view of the city and the port.

The original Inner Harbor master plan created over twenty years ago included a world-class
waterfront community with a marina, offices, homes, shops, a park and waterside promenade.
That vision is now becoming a reality at Inner Harbor East.

Representing a joint partnership between private developers and city and state planners,
this twenty acre, eight block development will offer businesses, residents and visitors alike
a distinctive neighborhood in which to work, shop and live.

Conveniently located across the street from Harborplace, and connected by walkways to the Convention Center and downtown offices, the **Hyatt Regency Baltimore** offers visitors a wide array of amenities in a casually elegant atmosphere. A spectacular glass and steel structure outside, the hotel's six-story atrium inside contains an oasis of lush greenery and a quiet waterfall. In addition to its 500 rooms and 25 suites, the Hyatt also has a rooftop restaurant and lounge which boasts a stunning view of the harbor.

ACCOMMODATIONS AND ENTERTAINMENT

Perhaps the dilemma of the seventh inning stretch at Baltimore's new Oriole Park at Camden Yards best exemplifies Baltimoreans' approach to having fun. No one can seem to decide on the music to broadcast over the loudspeaker while the fans are stretching for their beloved Orioles. Should it be the Beatles or John Denver's "Thank God I'm a Country Boy?" Fans love their big-city team, but many are in fact country people at heart. Baltimore natives just can't decide what they like best, so they do everything.

A summer weekend may include a fine French dinner at one of the many excellent hotel dining rooms scattered around the Inner Harbor, followed by a long night partying to country and western or old-time rock and roll in Fells Point. Maybe it's the spaghetti and ravioli dinner at St. Leo's in Little Italy and an evening on board one of the harbor cruise boats that will highlight a Sunday schedule. If the Orioles, the Blast, or the Skipjacks are in town, it's a sure bet that plenty of locals will be on hand to cheer. Of course, for many there's no better way to spend the afternoon than bent over a newspaper-covered table heaped with steaming, spicy, hard crabs, a wooden mallet in one's hand and a pitcher of beer at one's elbow.

Like everything else here, leisure is changing dramatically while somehow remaining the same. The opening of Harborplace brought a cosmopolitan air to a city which heretofore was pretty much a working-class town. Twenty years ago Baltimore was strictly a steak-and-seafood city, with a handful of ethnic eateries. Now one can find fine dining from all corners of the globe, for it seems as if an exciting new restaurant throws open its doors every week. The surprise is that the natives, long considered stuck in their ways, are trying all these new things and liking them.

The same can be said for other forms of leisure besides eating, although eating is still probably the favorite pastime in this city which Oliver Wendell Holmes once called the "gastronomic center of the universe." Pleasure boats flock to the Inner Harbor, sails fluttering on a horizon that not long ago was filled with little more than tugs and rusty old steamers. Retailing has changed since the days when the only place to shop was the four department stores at the corner of Howard and Lexington. Today, shops fill city streets and downtown plazas with designer fashions and safari gear, the newest electronic gadgetry, and crafts from as far away as the South Pacific.

Once, Baltimoreans went out of their way to avoid downtown, but now they swarm here year-round. When the weather is warm this is especially true, for the Inner Harbor and parks near it become a summer-long festival. Ethnic festivals fill calendars from May until the kids go back to school. Artscape, a celebration of Baltimore's role in the contemporary art scene, takes over the streets around The Maryland Institute for a weekend in July. The season is capped off with the Baltimore City Fair, a potpourri of games, rides, neighborhood and community displays and, of course, food.

Baltimore's many parks are frequently the scene of smaller celebrations of city living. It's difficult to find a neighborhood in the city that doesn't boast at least a handkerchief-sized patch of greenery, and the city is blessed with many larger parks. Many are the endowments of wealthy Baltimoreans who left their estates to be used as public parks. Indeed, the estate names remain in many cases: Druid Hill, Clifton, and Montebello.

Druid Hill Park is the city's largest, on several hundred acres in northwest Baltimore. The park has extensive groves of trees and lawns, a bandstand, a lake, and the Baltimore Zoo. The Zoo has undergone a major renovation and modernization, and now visitors can enjoy the Zoo's animals in settings similar to their natural habitats.

Patterson Park is the heart of East Baltimore's communities. Its pagoda stands on the hill where the British were repulsed in 1814. Today, Patterson Park has acres of lawns, a lake, and a swimming pool, together with baseball diamonds and athletic fields. In the summer the nearby neighborhood of Butcher's Hill sponsors a series of outdoor concerts that draw Baltimoreans from all across town for an evening picnic and everything musical from the Baltimore Symphony to ethnic dancing.

As visitors and Baltimoreans alike returned in droves to the city in the 1970's, the demand for new products, new pursuits, and new hotels grew. When the Baltimore Convention Center greeted its first guests in 1979 there were scarcely enough rooms available in town to house a convention of midget basketball stars. But within five or six years there were several thousand new rooms within an easy walk of the waterfront. The venerable Lord Baltimore was given a complete renovation to join the ranks of the glass-fronted Hyatt Regency, The Stouffer Harborplace Hotel, and the elegant Harbor Court. Other Baltimore establishments, including the world-famous Belvedere, were spruced up, and historic buildings were converted to hotels and guest houses.

So if a visitor's preference is an ultra-modern suite, he can choose the Marriott, the Omni, or the Sheraton. Maybe the intimacy of a guest house or a bed-and-breakfast inn is the choice. In that case, there's the Shirley House in Mount Vernon or the Admiral Fell Inn at the foot of Broadway in Fells Point.

Baltimore restaurants have come a long way from the fifties, when the typical fare was little more than steaks and chops, with the odd seafood entree thrown in. In Harborplace alone there are half-a-dozen restaurants featuring menus from the Orient, France, East India, and of course, the Maryland Eastern Shore.

But any guest who knows anything about Baltimore usually wants to try steamed crabs. The red-hot crustaceans have become the town's chief edible ambassador. H.L. Mencken wrote of the surprise of his New York friends when, upon arriving at his Hollins Street home for a "feast," they were led to the basement where a long table was covered with yesterday's Sunpapers and a bushel of steaming "jimmies" (large, heavy, male blue crabs).

After sundown the city takes on a different personality. The taverns of Fells Point feature hundreds of different varieties of beer and almost as many types of music. From country tunes at Ledbetter's to rock at On Broadway, music pulses into the narrow streets and alleys. In centuries past, Fells Point was the first dry land onto which visiting sailors stepped. The sailors are mostly gone but Fells Point remains the same.

There's no shortage of things to occupy one's time in this town. The trick, for someone here for but a short time, is to decide what to do. Be advised not to ask the advice of a Baltimorean, however. Locals can't even decide what kind of music they like during the ballgame.

The Radisson Plaza Lord Baltimore Hotel is a unique historic landmark located in the heart of downtown Baltimore. It is located just three blocks from the Inner Harbor and Oriole Park at Camden Yards. The Radisson Plaza has 440 beautifully restored guest rooms, a Plaza Club level, Cafe Royale Restaurant, the Oak Room Lobby Bar and a fitness center. Step back to a time when true grandeur, elegance and service existed with a visit to our hotel.

The Baltimore Marriott Inner Harbor is just a short walk from the Inner Harbor and the heart of the business district. Centrally located it has easy access to Interstate 95, it is only 12 minutes from Baltimore - Washington International Airport, within two blocks of the Convention Center and the Baltimore Arena, and Oriole Park at Camden Yards. The Baltimore Marriott is an ideal location for meetings, banquets, conventions, training sessions and seminars.

Harbor Court Hotel

Harbor Court Hotel

Haussner's

Overlooking Baltimore's spectacular Inner Harbor, the **Harbor Court Hotel** offers a world-class level of elegance that is virtually unparalleled. Enjoy exquisite dining in one of two four-star restaurants, Hampton's and Brightons. Beautiful appointed accommodations, and a fully-staffed and equipped Fitness Center are all yours to enjoy at the Harbor Court Hotel. As much a local institution as a restaurant, **Haussner's** has greeted diners at its Highlandtown location since 1926. The menu is extensive, featuring everything from crab cakes to sauerbraten to what is reputed to be the best strawberry pie on the east coast.

One of Baltimore's leading business hotels is the **Sheraton Inner Harbor Hotel**. Located one block from Harborplace and two blocks from Oriole Park at Camden Yards, the Sheraton is connected by a skywalk to the adjacent Baltimore Convention Center. The hotel features 337 spacious guest rooms, many with a view of the Inner Harbor, an Executive Level, indoor health club and pool, The Orioles Bar and McHenrys Restaurant offering an innovative sampler menu. The Sheraton is the Official Headquarters Hotel of the Baltimore Orioles.

43

Josef's

Peerces Plantation

Peerces Plantation is a restaurant for all Seasons - a restaurant for all Reasons.
A dining landmark for 52 years which overlooks scenic Loch Raven Reservoir. Serving continental cuisine
inside or on its new, year-round patio with a romantic fire place. **Josef's** brings the feeling and culinary
style of the Black Forest to Harford County. Josef's Restaurant has been chosen as one
of the Top 50 Continental Restaurants in the country for the last 3 years.

Lovingly restored to capture the bygone days of Baltimore's beginnings, the **Admiral Fell Inn** provides the best of old world charm and modern day conveniences. Surrounded by great clubs, eclectic shops and the spectacular sights of historic Fells Point, the Inn provides custom-styled rooms and a variety of dining options, all at the harbor's edge. It's English-style pub, famous restaurant, and romantic candlelit courtyard are favorites among those who have strolled the cobblestone streets at the Inn.

The Milton Inn

The Milton Inn

Days Hotel & Conference Center, Timonium

Located in a 240-year old fieldstone building in Northern Baltimore County, the **Milton Inn** creates one of the most romantic dining experiences in the area. Its wine cellar and renowned cuisine have bolstered the Milton Inn's tradition of excellence that began almost fifty years ago.
Days Hotel & Conference Center, Timonium is an extraordinary lodging alternative for business, convention and pleasure travellers. The glint of polished brass, the sparkle of chandeliers, the creams and beige hues of marble in the lobby, as well as consideration and hospitality, set the tone for your stay.

Since opening their doors in November of 1987, **The Sheraton Baltimore North**, located in the exclusive
suburb of Towson, has been offering a welcome relief to the excitement of downtown.
The Sheraton Baltimore North features 284 oversized deluxe rooms with in room coffeemakers,
first run movies, hospitality bars, indoor pool, health club and free parking. For your culinary delight
there is Carnegies Restaurant and the Outdoor Patio Cafe, or the exciting entertainment
in Warfield's Lounge and Nightclub.

47

Velleggia's

Da Mimmo

Situated between the Inner Harbor and Fell's Point, Little Italy is famed for its abundance of
fine restaurants and eateries. Two of the neighborhood's finest are Da Mimmo and Velleggia's.
Da Mimmo offers spectacular pasta dishes and an extensive menu of unique seafood and meat dishes
in an elegant atmosphere. **Velleggia's** is the oldest, family-owned restaurant in the Little Italy.
Opened in the 1930's as Enrico's Friendly Tavern, Velleggia's is a Baltimore landmark
known especially for its Saltimbocca and Calamari Marinara.

The Chart House is a dining treasure just waiting to be discovered at Baltimore's Inner Harbor.
Located on Pier 4, and almost hidden behind the new Mammal Pavilion, the red-brick restaurant features a
delectable menu in a casual, yet romantic, atmosphere. Filled with nautical memorabilia and ship models,
the Chart House also boasts a fantastic patio at the harbor's edge, where patrons can sip cool drinks on a
warm summer evening. The Chart House is definitely a restaurant worth searching for.

The Block

Stouffer Harborplace Hotel

Central Station

Bohager's Bar and Grill

The neon lights of Baltimore's infamous **Block** have lit up Baltimore Street for decades, offering countless adult clubs and entertainments for those who stroll down its sidewalks. **The Stouffer Harborplace Hotel**, connected to the Gallery at Harborplace, is one of the city's largest hotels. Stouffer Harborplace Hotel has 622 luxury rooms, the largest ballroom in the state, 18 meeting rooms and Windows Restaurant and Lounge. **Central Station** is one of Baltimore's most renowned neighborhood restaurants. Located in Mt. Vernon, it offers a broad menu and excellent service. Located in a warehouse that was once one of Baltimore's first breweries, **Bohager's Bar and Grill** captures a bygone era of great service and value.

Rock and roll fans from well beyond Maryland's borders come to **Hammerjacks**, Baltimore's best known night club. Featuring some of the world's most renowned rock acts, most notably heavy-metal bands and alternative music acts, Hammerjacks is also famous for highlighting many up-and-coming local acts trying to break into the "big time." Located in an old brewery near Oriole Park, the club recently built a state-of-the-art concert hall to accommodate larger crowds. Hammerjacks is still a major night spot for the blue-collar clientele it originally attracted, even though its crowds are now more socially diverse.

Obrycki's

Tio Pepe

Maryland Crabs

Tio Pepe

Eating steamed crabs at **Obrycki's** could be described as the purest of Baltimore's dining experiences.
One of the oldest crab houses in the city, Obrycki's is both sophisticated and fun at the same time.
Crack open a pile of steaming hot Maryland crabs and a wash it down with a frosty pitcher of beer,
served just the way Baltimoreans have done it for years. **Tio Pepe's**, near Mt. Vernon, is one of the city's
premier restaurants. Noted for its spectacular Spanish cuisine, and served in an intimate atmosphere,
Tio Pepe's is consistently rated one of Baltimore's finest restaurants.

The Culinary Arts Institute

The Inn at Government House

The Culinary Arts Institute

The Inn at Government House

Baltimore's **Culinary Arts Institute** is one of the region's best known schools for the training of
food service professionals. The school doubles as a restaurant, where students practice their crafts as chefs
and servers. **The Inn at Government House** recaptures the spirit of the 19th century with authentic
Victorian pieces, original period artwork and master-crafted replicas. The Government House is also used
as a training center for Baltimoreans developing careers in the hospitality industry.

The Baltimore Convention Center has attracted some of the nation's largest meetings and trade shows since its construction in 1979. Located just west of the Inner Harbor, the Center's facilities include Festival Hall, a huge exhibit space where some of the regions largest arts and crafts shows, antique exhibits and professional meetings are held. Recently, the Convention Center hosted the Upper Deck All-Star FanFest, a spectacular display of baseball memorabilia and interactive exhibits relating to the history of Major League Baseball.

54

Despite its current size and flexibility, plans have been approved to renovate and expand the
Baltimore Convention Center. Scheduled to be operative by the end of 1996, the new Convention Center
will include more than 302,000 square-feet of exhibit space and over 87,000 square-feet of meeting space.
A high-tech special presentation room with 500 permanent, tiered seats will also be added.
Once the Center is completed, the new convention space will accommodate
practically any size meeting or trade show, making Baltimore a leader in its field.

This elegant Victorian greenhouse, known as the Conservatory, is located in Druid Hill Park along with the Baltimore Zoo. Built in 1888, and sitting among colorful outdoor gardens, the Conservatory shelters a huge variety of exotic tropical plants and trees, including rubber, banana and palm trees. A display of desert and jungle plants are housed in greenhouses that are located nearby.

A favorite among children of all ages, the Baltimore Zoo is nestled among the 150-acre expanse of
Druid Hill Park. More than 1,200 species of mammals, birds and reptiles are on display here,
many in natural habitats and open-air environments. The third oldest zoo in the nation,
the Baltimore Zoo also features eighteen species of waterfowl on the old Boat Lake, which is a focal point of
the park. In recent years, the Zoo has expanded through the development of interactive exhibits
for children and programs that stress animal protection and environmental conservation.

The entire week before the running of the Preakness at Pimlico Race Track is filled with magnificent parties and events. One of the most popular spectacles during Preakness Week is the Balloon Race. Huge balloons of all colors and shapes dot the skies over Baltimore as they float free from the earth and head across the Chesapeake Bay to the Eastern Shore. The events of the week offer entertainment extravaganza's to all who simply love a good party.

One of the newer activities held during Preakness Week is the Balloon Glow. Brightly colored balloons - some traditionally shaped and some uniquely shaped to reflect the products of their sponsors - glow in the soft firelight burning from within the inflated balloons. The Balloon Glow is held on the rolling hills of Oregon Ridge Park, just north of the city. This unique visual delight is a real hit for those who have experienced it, and is sure to become a regular Preakness Week event.

59

The B & O Railroad Museum, at the Mount Clare Station, proudly represents Baltimore as the birthplace
of America's railroading history. Centered around an enormous roundhouse dating from 1884,
the museum boasts a plethora of restored railroad cars and locomotives. Mount Clare Station,
now part of the museum, has stood here since 1830. James Maccubbin Carroll, an heir to Charles Carroll
of Carrollton, one of the signers of the Declaration of Independence, gave land north of Mount Clare
for what was to be the first passenger station in America.

HISTORIC MONUMENTS

It is no coincidence that in the Baltimore City white pages there is a Monumental Life Insurance Company, a Monumental Uniform Company, Monumental Liquors and Monumental Savings and Loan. For over 150 years, Baltimore has been deservedly called the "Monumental City." Baltimoreans have memorialized everything from our first president to our humblest rowhouses in a monument or museum of one sort or another.

The first and still the most significant of these memorials is the Washington Monument, the shadow of which has made the daily round of Mount Vernon Place since its completion in 1829. Colonel John Eager Howard donated the site in "Howard's Woods" with a noble panorama of the city spread beneath it. It was so distant from town, city fathers concluded, that should the monument topple it would do little damage. On July 4, 1815, while "Professor" Bunzie's band played "Yankee Doodle," the artillery fired a one-hundred gun salute and the Most Worshipful Master of the Baltimore Masons laid the cornerstone. The tall marble column, unembellished yet beautiful in a kind of Doric simplicity, was designed by noted architect Robert Mills.

At nearly the same time a second monument was rising at the corner of Calvert and Lexington Streets. On September 12, 1815, Professor Bunzie was again on hand to herald the commencement of the Battle Monument, in memory of those Baltimoreans who had fallen the previous September when the British forces advanced upon the city.

From the time the two monuments were completed, they were models for the development of the areas around them. Mount Vernon Place has been compared with the finest urban squares in Europe, with its gracious dwellings facing a quiet park filled with the bronzes of Antoine Barye. Battle Monument Square sets a sober example for the lawyers who daily pass, for it is the centerpiece of the city's court and legal community.

Nearly every war in which Baltimoreans have participated has been commemorated in a local monument. A shaft with a female figure on top, at the corner of Cathedral Street and Mount Royal Avenue, recalls the Maryland Line, the state's Revolutionary War unit that was the backbone of Washington's army. The Civil War is also a popular subject for Baltimore sculptors. The Confederate Soldiers' and Sailors' Monument on Mount Royal Avenue is balanced by a similar monument to the armies of the North. Robert E. Lee and Stonewall Jackson are memorialized in Wyman Park and there is a monument to the women of the Confederacy on Charles Street.

Every Baltimore neighborhood has its monument to the fallen in the past two World Wars, and there are assorted statues of Edgar Allan Poe, Johns Hopkins, Mayor Latrobe, Cecilius Calvert, and Francis Scott Key. Among the city's most striking new monuments is the Holocaust Memorial, at Water and Gay Streets, which remembers those who perished in German concentration camps during World War II.

The Francis Scott Key Monument stands on the grounds of the Fort McHenry National Monument and National Shrine. Today, military life of the period is recreated with frequent Tattoos and parades. The restored powder magazine, guardroom, officers' quarters and barracks contain exhibits describing the life of the soldiers who fought here.

Local museums also bear witness to Baltimore's veneration of the past. The Peale Museum, now the centerpiece of the Baltimore City Life Museums, was the first museum in America when it opened in 1814. The Peale is a block from City Hall and contains a vast collection of Baltimore memorabilia. The second floor of the museum is given over to "Rowhouse," a display that celebrates rowhouse living in Baltimore for three centuries. This imaginative retrospective brings the museum into the realm of day-to-day Baltimore life, for nearly everyone in town has a rowhouse somewhere in his or her past.

At Lombard and Front Streets a collection of museums has grown around the Carroll Mansion, an 1811 townhouse in which Charles Carroll of Carrollton, one of Maryland's signers of the Declaration of Independence, died in 1832. These include The 1840 House, in which the day-to-day life of the family that occupied the humble brick dwelling is portrayed by actors cast in the roles as Irish immigrants. Next door is the Urban Archaeology Museum, with displays illustrating how archaeology aids in unraveling the city's past.

The Maryland Historical Society, near Mount Vernon, is the largest repository of Maryland memorabilia in the state. Its maritime museum memorializes the thousands of Marylanders who have worked the water, and the Darnall Young People's Museum gives children a hands-on historical experience. The period rooms are filled with Maryland furniture, paintings, silver, and decorative arts.

Many other museums keep Baltimore history alive. The Baltimore Industrial Museum displays a turn-of-the-century tailor shop like hundreds that employed immigrant tailors, an oyster-shucking plant and an early printing shop. The B&O Railroad Museum, housed in a century-old roundhouse on the site that is the birth of railroading in America, is an impressive collection of hundreds of locomotives and railroad cars. There's a public works museum, a dental museum, a firefighting museum, a streetcar museum, and even a museum of incandescent light bulbs. The USS Constellation, the oldest ship of the United States Navy, is docked at Harborplace, returning to the city of her birth after over 150 years at sea.

Homes of many famous Baltimoreans are open to the public. The H.L. Mencken House, in Union Square in West Baltimore, memorializes the work of the famous journalist. A tiny home on Amity Street was the residence of Edgar Allan Poe, and the garret in which he worked is furnished as it may have been during the mid-1800's. Another rowhouse, the home of the "Sultan of Swat," one-time Oriole Babe Ruth, contains a baseball museum second in size only to the Baseball Hall of Fame. A simple brick home on Paca Street was the home of Elizabeth Ann Seton, founder of the American parochial school system. Canonized in 1975, Mother Seton was the first American saint.

It's hard to draw the line about what is and what isn't a monument in Baltimore. Every rowhouse in every historic community is, in a sense, a memorial to the past. The "street arabs" who hawk produce up and down city alleys from horse-drawn wagons, the deck hands who work on the harbor tugs are no less monuments of a sort than are museums or statues. In Baltimore, the past has achieved almost reverential importance, and the city is certainly the better for it.

Rising above the gardens and flowering cherry trees of Mt. Vernon, the Washington Monument was the first
major monument erected to our first President. Built with funds collected through a public lottery,
the cornerstone was laid by the citizens of Baltimore on July 4, 1815. Designed by architect Robert Mills,
the marble monument was recently restored and opened to the public. A small room
at the top of the shaft allows visitors to take in a panoramic view of the city.

During the middle of the nineteenth century, the Washington Monument was the centerpiece of one
of Baltimore's most fashionable neighborhoods, Mt. Vernon. Currently, along tree-lined streets,
the neighborhood is the home of many exciting museums, historic homes and fine restaurants,
including the Walters Art Gallery, the Peabody Conservatory and the Hackerman House.
The area is also renowned for its unique shopping and fine galleries.

Fort McHenry, the birthplace of Francis Scott Key's Star Spangled Banner, was the final barrier to the Baltimore harbor in the War of 1812. Reenactments of the historic 24-hour battle still take place at the fort, which was bombarded by the British on September 13, 1814. Key penned the National Anthem from a British ship anchored in the harbor, where he was being held captive anchored in the harbor during the battle. A replica of the flag that inspired the anthem flies from the fort.

The star-shaped walls of Fort McHenry lie at water's edge, where it defended the city from British attack during the War of 1812. From the air, one can see out onto the harbor, where dozens of pleasure boats escort the Pride of Baltimore II toward the Chesapeake on another adventure to foreign lands. The fort is one of Baltimore's most historic, and popular, sites.

Mount Clare

Evergreen Mansion

Mount Clare

Blacks in Wax Museum

Begun in 1756, Mount Clare was the home of Charles Carroll, a Barrister, and a cousin of one of the signers of the Declaration of Independence. A registered National Historic Landmark, this first historic museum house in Maryland opened in 1917. Located on North Charles Street, Evergreen House is a beautiful Mid-19th Century mansion. Maintained amid manicured and lush grounds, the mansion houses numerous art treasures. The Blacks in Wax is an "eye-opening" newcomer to the museum scene.
"Life-like" wax figures of great blacks of Maryland, the United States, and of the World are on display.

The Baltimore Streetcar Museum recalls a time in Baltimore when the streets were filled with tracks and trolleys. In 1965, the last streetcar was retired, although some would say the idea of streetcars is making a comeback with Baltimore's modern light-rail system. The museum features displays and films on the history of streetcars, as well as exciting rides that take us back a century or more to the way Baltimore used to be.

Maryland Historical Society

The Star Spangled Flag House

All types of Maryland memorabilia are cataloged and displayed at the Maryland Historical Society,
which was created in 1844. Portraits, furniture, clothing and maritime artifacts all remind us of Maryland's
historic past. The Star Spangled Banner House is the home where Mary Pickersgill stitched
the flag that flew over Fort McHenry, and which inspired the writing of Francis Scott Key's
"Star Spangled Banner." The historic home is restored and furnished to capture
the authentic flavor of the Federal period.

The Bromo Seltzer Tower

The Shot Tower

The "Bromo Seltzer Tower," where the indigestion remedy was originally created, is now the home
of the Mayor's Advisory Council on Arts and Culture. In years gone by, it was topped by a 51-foot,
blue Bromo Seltzer bottle. The Shot Tower was where molten lead was poured through sieves
and into vats of cold water below. The lead shot was then used by soldiers and hunters for ammunition.
The 234-foot brick tower is one of the city's most unique landmarks, and
it is located just northeast of the Inner Harbor.

The Carroll Mansion – City Life Museums

The Edgar Allan Poe House

Carroll Mansion and Courtyard Sites – City Life Museums

Peale Museum – City Life Museums

Four of Baltimore's most overlooked, but most intriguing historic sites include the Edgar Allan Poe House, and the Peale Museum, the Carroll Mansion and Courtyard Sites at the City Life Museums. The Poe House is where the famous writer supposedly penned some of his most notable works between 1832 and 1835. The Carroll Mansion is the home of one of the signers of the Declaration of Independence, who lived here until 1832. Costumed staff at the City Life Museums recreate life as it was lived in the early 19th century. The Peale Museum holds a diverse collection of portraits and artifacts, including fossils and famous paintings by Baltimore's Peale family.

The Babe Ruth Museum

The Babe Ruth Museum

The H.L. Mencken House

With a resurgence of interest in America's favorite pastime, the Babe Ruth museum is a must see
for any visitor to the city. Displays devoted to the "Sultan of Swat," who was born
in this narrow rowhouse, can be seen here, as well as exhibits celebrating the Orioles, the Baltimore Colts
football team, and other famous Baltimore sports heroes. Henry Louis Mencken, the Baltimore journalist
and cultural critic from the early days of the 20th century, lived in this spacious rowhouse on
the historic Union Square. His second floor office is meticulously restored, and a local actor gives tours
of the house while lambasting the rich and famous of Mencken's day.

Trains from steam locomotives to sleek modern-looking engines grace the yards at the B&O Railroad Museum, located just blocks from the Inner Harbor. Centered around an original 1844 roundhouse, the museum pays tribute to the birth of American railroading in Baltimore with an extensive collection of train memorabilia. A massive model train exhibit at the museum is also a favorite among visitors.

A sleek engine roars by in the imaginations of visitors of the B&O Railroad Museum.
With dozens of cars and locomotives on display inside and outside of its historic roundhouse,
the museum is a favorite among children. The nation's first passenger depot, the Mount Clare Station,
was begun in 1830 and is also part of the museum. An heir of Maryland's famous Carroll family
gave land north of the Mount Clare estate to the B&O Railroad in 1831, and track was laid nearby
for the first passenger line in the United States.

73

The Walters Art Gallery

The stunning marble columns of the Walters Art Gallery beckon visitors inside from its main entrance
on Charles Street. Rooms off of this center hallway lead to a variety of paintings and sculptures
collected in Europe and Asia by William Walters during the 19th century. An addition, built in 1974,
allows the Walters to present films, lectures and other performances, making it
one of the leaders in Baltimore's art and cultural scenes.

THE ARTS

As motorists approach Baltimore, fighting the traffic to Mulberry Street, art is probably secondary to getting to the office on time. Yet here, on the brick wall of a rowhouse where one would least expect, it is a monumental painting. Billboard-like in its scale, it depicts a pair of elderly Baltimoreans hunched over a checkerboard on some city sidewalk. Not only does the painting by Baltimore artist James Voshell capture a bit of Baltimore life, it also sets the stage for the art scene here: expect the unexpected.

For Baltimore is not a city born into the arts. There is no Soho, no enclave where artists from around the world gather to set international trends. Yet don't assume that Baltimore has no foundation of culture. Not only are all aspects of both the visual and the performing arts well represented in Baltimore, but art here saturates life down to street level, or at least just above street level in the case of the many wall paintings like Mr. Voshell's.

In even the most exalted collections there is a special sort of Baltimore link. The Walters Art Gallery, on Mount Vernon Place, has its basis in the collections of merchant William Walters. Walters spent the Civil War in Paris, where he rubbed shoulders with Corot, Daumier, and their counterparts. He began to collect European and Asian art, from paintings to porcelain to Medieval armor. His son Henry continued to expand the collection. Though either the father or the son could easily have moved to major cultural centers like New York or Paris, they chose to keep their artistic wealth here in Baltimore.

The story of one of Baltimore's most important collections, the Cone Collection in the Baltimore Museum of Art, is much the same. The Cone sisters, Claribel and Etta, made some thirty trips to Europe after 1900 where they made friends with Matisse, Picasso and their friends. They began buying the artists' works when no one else was interested in them, works that were little understood in conservative Baltimore.

With its move to the Baltimore Museum of Art in 1949, the Cone Collection testified to the city's artistic awakening, for in her will Claribel had specified that "unless the spirit of appreciation of modern art" showed evidence of growth in Baltimore, the collection should go elsewhere. It stayed in Baltimore, complementing an already-impressive collection of American paintings, period rooms, silver and furniture in the classical Baltimore Museum of Art building. A 1982 addition increased the museum's ability to display its collections, and an outdoor sculpture garden completes the panorama along Art Museum Drive.

The art history of Maryland has its home at the Maryland Historical Society just blocks from Mount Vernon Place. The Society's collection includes portraits of three centuries of prominent Marylanders as well as the enormous Robert G. Merrick collection of Maryland historic prints.

Since its birth in 1826, the Maryland Institute of Art has displayed the work of established artists as well as emerging and student artists. The white marble facade of the main building has been a fixture on Mount Royal Avenue for well over a hundred years. The Institute has aggressively sought other buildings, including the old Mount Royal train station and a defunct shoe factory, converting them to classroom and studio space.

After Charles Center was completed, North Charles Street slowly became the gallery center of Baltimore. A dozen or so private galleries dot the street in the area around Mount Vernon Place, displaying everything from crafts to folk art to contemporary works.

Yet beyond the galleries lies the art of the streets of Baltimore. Just walk down Patterson Park Avenue on a summer day to see Baltimore's most famous indigenous art form: painted window screens depicting cool, mountainous rural scenes. Or take note of the sculptures in front of so many Baltimore schools, part of the city's "1% for Art Program." So much for Baltimore's ancient reputation as a blue-collar, cultural wasteland.

The same can be said for the concert halls and the theatres that play to Baltimore audiences. The Baltimore Symphony Orchestra, whose home is the monumental Joseph Meyerhoff Symphony Hall, has carved a place as a world-class orchestra with concert tours to Europe and the Soviet Union. The Meyerhoff is one of the finest halls in the country, a room so successful that its opening was heralded with a one-hour special on National Public Television simply to describe how it was "tuned" for acoustical perfection.

Since 1895 the Lyric Opera House, home of the Baltimore Opera, has hosted the country's leading virtuosos. The fine old theatre, recently renovated, continues to present not only opera, but ballet and a variety of theatrical performances and cinema. The hall retains the grandeur of the turn of the century, every bit the equal of some of the finest opera houses in Europe.

Mount Vernon Place has become sort of a cultural mecca in Baltimore, largely due to the presence of the Peabody Institute, Baltimore's nationally-recognized conservatory of music. For years the Peabody has been the center of the city's musical life, bringing many of the world's most famous artists here to teach or perform.

Baltimore's Morris A. Mechanic Theatre, which presents Broadway plays and musicals, is rooted in decades of popular musical tradition. Mechanic was the manager of Ford's Theatre when George M. Cohan and Tallulah Bankhead performed there. Lillian Russell, Ethel Barrymore, and Al Jolson appeared in local Vaudeville theatres, and today's Mechanic hosts the country's leading Broadway stars.

Just steps from Mount Vernon Place, Center Stage is the Maryland State Theatre, presenting everything from Shakespeare to Kurt Vonnegut. For over twenty years Center Stage has challenged Baltimoreans with the work of new, talented playwrights and has pioneered updated, daring productions of theatrical classics.

Smaller theatres across Baltimore, including the Arena Stage and a host of repertory companies like the Vagabonds assure that theatre is accessible to everyone who enjoys the smell of greasepaint. There is a long history of small theatre in the port city, enabling daytime homemakers or accountants to become Juliet, Cyrano, or Willy Loman when the stage lights come up.

But this should be no surprise. Art seems to pervade much of Baltimore life. Ask Baltimore moviemaker John Waters. His popular films often feature the beehive hairdos of East Baltimore and the not-so-lyrical twang of a Highlandtown waitress. Waters finds art everywhere he looks - down narrow city alleys or inside formstone-fronted rowhouses. Maybe Waters is just more perceptive than most Baltimoreans, but in this town of merchant ships and corner taverns one need not look too hard to find Baltimore's particular sort of culture.

The Baltimore Museum of Art

The Baltimore Museum of Art, Sculpture Garden

The Baltimore Museum of Art, Sculpture Garden

The Baltimore Museum of Art

The Baltimore Museum of Art is home to many collections, most notably the Cone Collection.
Bequeathed by Etta and Claribel Cone, who made dozens of trips to Europe at the beginning
of the 20th century, the collection boasts a huge catalog of work by Henri Matisse.
The museum also displays a wide variety of modern and contemporary art,
a large collection of furniture and decorative arts, and an expanded sculpture garden
which rests in a peaceful, tree-filled lot just east of the museum.

The Baltimore Museum of Art

Rising from a small hill above Wyman Park, the Baltimore Museum of Art is the best place to see great works of modern and contemporary art by Cezanne, Renoir, Warhol and Motherwell. After the sun goes down, a display of challenging contemporary neon art can be seen on the wall of an east wing. Located near Johns Hopkins University, the museum also presents a wide variety of films, lectures and performances that are especially popular among Baltimore's art aficiandos.

The Walters Art Gallery–Main Building

The Walters Art Gallery–Main Building

The Walters Art Gallery–Main Building

The Walters Art Gallery–Main Building

The Walters Art Gallery, located in Mt. Vernon near the Washington Monument, is truly an inspiring space
in which to see a wide variety of paintings, sculpture and tapestries from ancient times to the present.
Several rooms downstairs offer a stunning exhibit of Egyptian art and armament artifacts,
including ancient weaponry and suits of armor. Much of the museum's Asian art is now displayed
in the Hackerman House, which was recently opened, and which is connected to the Gallery.

The Walters Art Gallery–Hackerman House

Recently opened in a beautiful mansion in Mt. Vernon, the Hackerman House is the home of
many beautiful works of Asian art, including paintings, carvings and decorative arts. This delicate
spiraling staircase leads to the second floor, where spectacularly restored rooms act as galleries
for the impressive displays. The collection is part of the Walters Art Gallery, and the two are connected
by a walkway that crosses between the two museums.

The Maryland Institute–Mount Royal Station

The Maryland Institute–Mount Royal Station

The Maryland Institute–Main Building

The Maryland Institute–Main Building

Since its inception in 1826, the Maryland Institute of Art has displayed the artwork of renowned artists, as
well as the work of the students it trains. The Mount Royal Station, now part of the Institute,
is an old railroad station that was bought and converted into studios, classrooms and galleries.
The station has become the centerpiece of Baltimore's famous ArtScape, which is a yearly celebration
to the Baltimore art scene. At ArtScape, writers, musicians and artists from many fields
feature their work for a weekend every summer.

The Peabody Conservatory

The Peabody Conservatory—Library

The Peabody Conservatory, located in Mount Vernon near the Walters Art Gallery and the Washington
Monument, is a world renowned center for the study of music. Created by merchant George Peabody in 1866,
the Peabody boasts a huge library, classes in dance and, of course, music. The architecture, both inside
and out, is exquisite, and even those with no musical talents would surely enjoy a visit
to the conservatory to see its beautiful "nooks and crannies."

With its curved white walls, its hanging acoustical deflectors and its graceful, intimate boxes,
the Joseph Meyerhoff Symphony Hall is state-of-the-art when it comes to acoustical design.
The $10.5 million Meyerhoff is home to the Baltimore Symphony Orchestra, whose growing reputation
both in the United States and in Europe, is appreciated by local concert-goers here in Baltimore.

Led by visionary conductor David Zinman, the world-class reputation of the Baltimore Symphony Orchestra has grown by leaps and bounds both in America and abroad. Under Zinman's tutelage, the Symphony has lured famous musicians to Baltimore for countless evenings of musical magic. The B.S.O. has also expanded many of its programs, multiplied its classical recordings, and toured to enthusiastic crowds all over Europe and the former Soviet Union.

The Lyric Opera House

Morris A. Mechanic Theatre

Morris A. Mechanic Theatre

The Lyric Opera House, home of the Baltimore Opera, has been host to some of the world's
most famous virtuosos. This old theatre, built in 1895, was recently renovated to its original
turn of the century splendor, and rivals some of Europe's finest. The Morris A. Mechanic Theatre is home
to some of Baltimore's finest productions of plays and musicals, many of which are Broadway bound.
This modern-shaped theatre was built in 1964, at the beginning of Baltimore's renaissance, and
has been host to some of the city's finest performances.

Center Stage

Located just footsteps from Mount Vernon, Center Stage presents great theatre ranging from
Shakespeare to O'neill to contemporary work by emerging artists. Plays are performed here
in two theatres, the Pearlstone Theatre on the main floor, and the recently added Head Theatre upstairs.
Both spaces are intimate and comfortable, and the Head Theatre is constructed in a way that allows
the theatre space to be adapted to the needs of the play that is being performed on its boards.

One of Baltimore's oldest neighborhoods, Fells Point was once a bustling port of entry. As a testament to the neighborhood's age, over 200 homes from the mid-1700's still stand in the neighborhood today, and some of the old brick warehouses line the water's edge just as they did during the birth of the city. Today, water taxis travel back and forth from the Inner Harbor, where visitors can take in the Broadway Market and a host of taverns, restaurants, galleries and shops that line the streets. Some of Baltimore's most interesting and eclectic "characters" hang out here, making people-watching a favorite pastime.

NEIGHBORHOODS

At first there were but three neighborhoods - Jonestown, Fells Point, and Baltimore Town. What would emerge as the city of Baltimore was the result of the blending of these three as they simply grew together. That single fact, the mingling of three towns into one, set the stage for the social growth of a city that today remains little more than a collection of neighborhoods.

The neighborhood identification is so strong that, were a visitor to Baltimore to ask a resident of Eastern Avenue where he lived, the answer would more likely be Highlandtown than Baltimore. Parish members at St. Leo's think of themselves first as neighbors in Little Italy and second as Baltimoreans. The same goes for those who scrub their white marble steps in Canton, march in the American Day Parade in Locust Point, play pick-up basketball in Harlem Park, toss a lacrosse ball around in Roland Park, and relax on benches in Mount Vernon.

Despite the glitz of the Inner Harbor it is the small neighborhoods that are the real heart of Baltimore, and it is the neighborhoods that give the city its distinctive character. Many are ethnic in nature, usually identifiable by the restaurants that dot the streets - Greek along Eastern Avenue, Chinese on Park Avenue, Italian on Albermarle Street. Even a language, or at least a dialect, "Baltimorese," has grown on neighborhood streets. In Waverly, residents wash dishes in the "zinc," and everyone in "Bawlamer" heads "downyashun" (translation: down the ocean) for vacation.

Other neighborhoods grew up around a market. Union Square is but blocks away from the Hollins Market which preceded it. South Baltimore and Federal Hill houses surround the Cross Street Market, and the Broadway Market is the focal point of Fells Point. Baltimore's market system is unique, a network of open markets in which small businesspeople rent stalls to sell everything from local produce to exotic coffee and tea. In many respects the Baltimore markets have changed little in over two centuries.

In fact, in many Baltimore neighborhoods this resistance to physical change, spawned by an honest respect for the history of the neighborhood, has been the catalyst to drive the area into the future. For some, such as Stirling Street, history has been the incentive to turn around what had become an economic and social downward spiral. In others, like Little Italy, the neighborhood tradition has continued unabated for generations, allowing it to grow and thrive into the twentieth century.

Several Baltimore neighborhoods are recognized by inclusion on the National Register of Historic Places and others have become local historic districts. Renovators in these historic neighborhoods are encouraged to return their houses to their early appearance and retain the architectural features which give them their character.

Baltimore neighborhoods have withstood tremendous social pressure in the last thirty years, and yet many survive with much the same temperament as generations ago. The key has been moving into the future with an eye to the neighborhood's past. A combination of contemporary urban revitalization techniques, historic preservation, and simple neighborhood pride has resulted in an urban rebirth unmatched by any city in the United States.

Many locally-grown ideas have spread to other cities. The Urban Homesteading, or "Dollar House" program turned thousands of abandoned houses into modern, comfortable dwellings. Baltimore came to the forefront of American preservation by creating the Commission for Historical and Architectural Preservation in 1964. Other revolutionary home ownership programs, inventive ways to finance private home buying and restoration, and successful ventures to turn dilapidated commercial buildings into apartments and condominiums have made Baltimore the national leader in neighborhood development.

A strong partnership between residents, the local government, and private business has encouraged change for the better throughout Baltimore. Individual community preservation organizations like the Society for the Preservation of Federal Hill and Fells Point or the Union Square Association have taken active parts in saving important structures, returning their neighborhoods to their past glory, and infusing a sense of community pride into residents who have taken on individual home restoration projects. The Citizens Planning and Housing Association has been working for responsible government in the areas of planning, housing, and zoning for more than forty years. Other organizations like the Neighborhood Housing Service have dedicated themselves to helping renters become homeowners, and private industry has joined the effort with innovative programs like Baltimore Gas and Electric's low-cost Home Winterization Program.

For the casual visitor, it may be difficult to penetrate the neighborhood soul of the city. Neighborhoods are distinctly different from each other, often in ways that are clearly visible. The popular painted window screens of East Baltimore, the stately brownstone facades of Mount Vernon, and the pristine garden fronts of Charles Village differentiate one neighborhood from another.

The one thing most neighborhoods have in common is the rowhouse. The humble brick rowhouses of eighteenth century Fells Point are the earliest examples in Baltimore. As the city prospered, its rowhouses became more spacious and elegant, yet they still shared their side walls with their neighbors in long, unbroken rows. Suburban developers have taken to calling them "townhouses," but in Baltimore City there is a sort of reverse-chic in living in what one proudly calls a rowhouse.

In many respects, one discovers precisely what has made Baltimore a modern, progressive city by visiting the neighborhoods that seem to pass through the ages virtually unchanged. Life here revolves around community activities like church suppers and summer street festivals. People stay in their respective neighborhoods because they like the feeling of identifying with something worthwhile. Increasingly, transplants from surrounding suburbs are returning to inner city neighborhoods because they find something here - a sense of fellowship, perhaps, or the satisfaction that comes from preserving something worth preserving - that is missing in tract house developments and garden apartments.

When out-of-towners talk about the great "Baltimore Renaissance" of the 1970's and 1980's they are usually talking about that part of the city's revitalization most easily observable: the clearing away of rotting piers to create the new Inner Harbor or the proliferation of new restaurants and entertainment centers. The real revitalization of the city, however, is taking place along the streets of its dozens of neighborhoods. Of course, maybe it's not a rebirth at all. Maybe Baltimore has always been a comfortable place to live.

Within easy walking distance from the Inner Harbor, Mt. Vernon is one of Baltimore's most exciting neighborhoods. The Washington Monument is the centerpiece for some of the city's finest brownstone and brick residences that face the Square. The neighborhood is probably best known for being the home of the Walters Art Gallery, the Peabody Conservatory and the Hackerman House, but other fine buildings, restaurants and galleries line the streets of the neighborhood, making it a great place for a weekend walk.

Long considered Baltimore's most prestigious neighborhood, the fine homes that face Mt. Vernon Place
date back to the early 1800's. These beautiful homes, including the Thomas-Jencks-Gladding House and the
1884 Engineering Society (the residence of railroad millionaire Robert Garrett), look out on Mt. Vernon
Square, which is a tree-filled park with fine sculpture and fountains. Every spring, the neighborhood
is laced with the sights and scents of flowering trees and gardens, which line the streets leading up to the
Washington Monument at the center of the park.

Village of Cross Keys

Guilford

Roland Park

Guilford

Named after a village that was once nearby, Cross Keys is a neighborhood designed by famous planner
James Rouse. Sophisticated architecture sits among wide open spaces here at the northern edge of the city.
Roland Park is also located at the city's edge. It is well-known for being one of the nation's
first planned communities, and it boasts the first shopping center in the country as well. Its well
manicured lawns and tree-lined streets reflect the influence of Frederick Law Olmstead,
the designer of Central Park in New York, and the Capitol grounds in Washington, D.C.

Guilford

Many of Baltimore's most luxurious homes can be found below the shadows of tall trees and lush foliage in Guilford, a community dating to just after World War I. Concepts originally utilized in building Guilford are often used today in residential neighborhoods: planning for parks, local organizing to prevent commercial zoning and assessments for maintenance. One of the highlights of Guilford is Sherwood Gardens, a spacious area of colorful flowers and shrubbery that was originally created by a single family. Originally maintained privately, the community now maintains the Gardens as a gift to the residents of the entire city.

91

Fells Point

Fells Point

Fells Point

Most Baltimoreans know of the charm and local flavor of the pubs and restaurants that crowd the streets of Fells Point. However, this neighborhood is also filled with eclectic shops, galleries and stores that offer everything from fine antiques to leftovers from the attic. And on nights and weekends, the streets come alive with excitement, making Fells Point one of the city's oldest neighborhoods that still seems to bring out the youth in anyone who strolls it brick-paved streets.

East Baltimore

Ridgely's Delight

East Baltimore

Otterbein

In East Baltimore, Patterson Park is a proud neighborhood of marble steps, painted screens and
well-kept streets. Surrounding a huge park that is famous for its soccer and softball tournaments,
Patterson Park is also known for its famous Chinese-style observatory, known simply as the "Pagoda."
During the 1970's, many of the homes and storefronts in Otterbein, just a short distance from
the Inner Harbor, were beautifully restored to their Federal period granduer.
Nearby, in Ridgely's Delight, rowhouses reflecting an Italian architectural influence,
were built by medical professionals who originally populated the area.

93

Edwardian rowhouses line the tree-shaded streets of Charles Village, some 30-odd blocks north of the Inner Harbor. Once known as Peabody Heights, Charles Village offers a unique mix of suburban delights in an urban setting. Well-kept yards and beautiful gardens are just some of the highlights in this neighborhood that is the home to Johns Hopkins University, the Baltimore Museum of Arts and Memorial Stadium. The unique architecture here features homes with large porches, columned parlors and ornate interiors.

Surrounding the Lyric Opera House, the Meyerhoff Symphony Hall and the Maryland Institute of Art, Bolton Hill is one of Baltimore's most elegant neighborhoods. F. Scott Fitzgerald, Gertrude Stein and the Cone sisters all once lived here, and Bolton Hill is still a favorite residence for those interested in the arts and humanities. Brick rowhouses of various styles line the streets and look out on tree-filled squares that are dotted with fountains and flowers. Every summer, on Mt. Royal Avenue, one of the neighborhood's main thoroughfares, Baltimore celebrates the arts with ArtScape, a weekend-long festival featuring local artists, writers and musicians.

Stirling Street

Federal Hill

Seton Hill

South Baltimore

Stirling Street was the first attempt in the nation at "urban homesteading," where twenty-five "dollar homes" were successfully saved from abandonment and decay. Seton Hill, dating to the 1790's, takes its name from the first American-born saint, Elizabeth Ann Seton. Its history dates to an order of French priests who first lived there. Dating to the beginning of the city, Federal Hill is filled with restored historic homes. South Baltimore is a conglomerate of smaller neighborhoods of proud working class families and eclectic shops.

Centered around a one square block park in southwest Baltimore, Union Square is a historic neighborhood dating to before the Civil War. H.L. Menken's house faces the square here, and many of the homes nearby have been meticulously restored to reflect their original appearance. Some are proudly put on display during annual festivals that neighborhood associations organize. Nearby, the Hollins Market area attracts local artists and craftspeople. The Sowebo festival is held here every summer, and huge crowds stop by to enjoy a wide variety of food, performances and artwork that is created by local artists.

Mt. Washington

Dickeysville

Coldspring

Dickeysville

Rural in setting, Mt. Washington shows off some of the finest homes of the Victorian era that were once country retreats for city residents of wealth. A small pocket of fine shops and restaurants currently attract crowds to this neighborhood of tall trees and expansive yards. Coldspring was designed by world-famous architect Moshe Safdie, and is a fine example of modern neighborhood planning. Dickeysville is a haven of narrow streets and clapboard houses that recalls a time past when city life was peaceful and slow.

Built of stone from local quarries, Hamden is one neighborhood in Baltimore that has resisted
the economic and environmental changes of the city. Overlooking the Jones Falls, which provided power
for several fabric mills in the area, these humble rowhouses were inhabited by the millworkers who
labored nearby. Today, at Mill Center, a community of local artists and craftspeople utilizes
some of the old mill buildings that still stand for studios and shops.

Edmondson Village

Hamilton

West Baltimore

West Baltimore

Northeast Baltimore, which includes Hamilton, has a wide variety of neighborhoods that at times feel urban and at times suburban. Full of parks and open green spaces, Northeast Baltimore reaches all the way to the Baltimore city border. West Baltimore is a mix of several stunning neighborhoods, such as Edmondson Village (which has a history dating to the Revolution), Lafayette Square, Harlem Park, West Arlington and the historic Walbrook, which dates to 1669.

Once an industrial community of decaying docks and old warehouses, Canton is now
one of Baltimore's poshest neighborhoods. On the harbor, just east of Fells Point,
a new waterfront area has been constructed, complete with marinas, condominiums and spacious
rowhomes that rise from the water's edge. Canton is just another example of the expansion of
Baltimore's urban renaissance that began in the late sixties and continues unabated today.

With spectacular Opening Day ceremonies, baseball fans in Baltimore and from all over the country celebrated the opening of the new stadium at Camden Yards in 1992. Meticulously designed and constructed to create the atmosphere of old ballparks, but with modern amenities, fans have flocked in record numbers to "The Yards" to watch Baltimore's pride and joy, the Orioles, battle American League foes for a trip to the World Series. In July 1993, Baltimore showed off its new gem by hosting the Major League All-Star game.

SPORTS AND RECREATION

It's July 13, 1993: a typically hot summer evening in downtown Baltimore. But tonight is different. There's a buzz of excitement in the air. The crowds milling around Harborplace seem to be walking a little faster and talking a little louder. Celebratory lights sparkle and glow from every window and street-lamp imaginable. After a thirty-five year wait, Baltimore finally plays host to the Major League All-Star game at the city's internationally acclaimed ballpark at Camden Yards. The locals may not be quite accustomed to the glitz and the glamor of the national attention, but they do know their baseball. With the game pretty much locked away in the win column, All-Star Oriole pitcher Mike Mussina gets up in the bullpen to loosen up, even though he knows he won't get into the game. But the fans at the game aren't aware of this and, in unison, they rise to their feet and begin to chant their local hero's name: "Mike, Mike, Mike."

Sports reporters, television announcers and fans from around the country cannot believe the clamor as the sound reverberates from the warehouse wall in deep right field. The din grows louder and louder, pulsing like a strange heartbeat, and continues until after the game when Mussina crosses the field and tips his cap in appreciative recognition.

What the announcers, reporters and other out-of-towners may not have realized, before this raucous civic demonstration, is the extent of the city's almost religious devotion to its sports teams. Certainly Baltimoreans recognize this kind of ardent enthusiasm. Back in the Sixties and Seventies, during Colts games at Memorial Stadium, crowd noise from the end zone used to be so loud that players couldn't hear themselves in their huddles. The floors at the Baltimore Arena shake like thunder from thousands of fans stomping and shouting during every Baltimore Spirit soccer game. Even sweaty high school gyms all over the city rock to the rhythms of basketballs and high-top sneakers during weekend contests. You see, Baltimoreans take their sports seriously.

When Oriole Park was being built at Camden Yards, just a few blocks from the city's famous Inner Harbor, there was a popular movie refrain that was repeated over and over - on the radio, on television, even in the streets: "If you build it, they will come." But no one, except maybe Baltimore sports fans, could have been prepared for just how many did come. After selling out a record setting sixty-five Oriole games in a row (the streak ended on a cold, rainy April night), a new streak of sell-outs was promptly begun. From its first opening day, zealots from all over the nation have converged on this new base-ball mecca, and for good reason. Designed with all the modern conveniences in mind, Oriole Park is nostalgically reminiscent of classic old ballparks. The "Yard" is built around a natural grass diamond with outfield walls set at quirky angles, tall old-fashioned scoreboards that flash the latest scores from every game, and finishing details that are still being discovered. The signature of this great ballpark, though, may be its red brick warehouse that reaches out into right-center field. Mammoth in size, the old B&O Railroad warehouse was to be an instant target for classic home run swingers trying to reach its win-dows with soaring fly balls. The warehouse also holds shops, eateries and clubs that stretch along a spacious walkway lined with old-time banners, flags, and of course, Boog Powell's famous ribs stand. This stadium truly is a "field of dreams," and Baltimoreans are justifiably proud of the structure, and the players who grace its green fields on those magic nights from April to October.

Since 1954, when a Major League team returned to Baltimore, the franchise has been one of the most successful in sports history. The team has won three World Series, six pennants, and has been involved in some of the most exciting pennant races in league history. Many great Oriole players have raced around the base paths, at Memorial Stadium and Camden Yards; Hall-of-Famers like Brooks Robinson, Frank Robinson, Jim Palmer and future Hall-of-Famers like Cal Ripken, Jr.

But as much as we love the "O's," Baltimore certainly shouldn't be thought of as a one sport town. Listen to local radio talk shows and you'll still hear callers debating fiercely over the great old Colts football teams who battled NFL foes at Memorial Stadium. When retired players like Johnny Unitas and Artie Donovan make personal appearances around town, crowds of avid Colts fans show up to meet their heroes. Most would swear they hear the sounds of the Colt's Marching Band swirling and echoing around in their heads.

For years, just like football, soccer has been a popular sport around the city. Even now, one can still take a walk down to Patterson Park in East Baltimore and watch some of the greatest league action to be seen. When a professional indoor soccer league was formed over a decade ago, fans packed the Civic Center (now the Baltimore Arena) to cheer on the home team. That team, the Blast, was one of the most successful franchises in the Major Indoor Soccer League, and the town developed an instant love affair with the team's players, and their coach, Kenny Cooper. The Blast are gone now, but a new league, and a new team, the Spirit, continue to attract screaming throngs to the Arena for exciting indoor soccer.

The Baltimore Arena also hosts many other major sports. The Washington Bullets play several NBA basketball games a year there, and the National Gymnastic Olympic Trials took place at the Arena recently, to great reviews and fanfare.

Another sport that is incredibly popular in Baltimore is lacrosse. Originally played by Native Americans, lacrosse took root here in the 1870's. Played with a hard ball that is cradled in a stick with a webbed pocket at one end, lacrosse is the rage at local colleges and universities like Johns Hopkins, Loyola and Towson State. The Baltimore Athletic Club fielded the first American team in the sport, and intense rivalries still exist among the many local lacrosse clubs in and around the city. Although the sport is taking hold in other parts of the country, particularly New England, Baltimore is still recognized as the heart and soul of lacrosse country.

The Baltimore area is also renowned for its equestrian sports. Probably best known among these is horse racing's second leg of the Triple Crown, the Preakness, held at Pimlico Race Course each May. Dating back to a thorough-bred race in 1873, the Preakness, along with the Kentucky Derby and the Belmont Stakes, is one of the most distinguished horse races in the world.

Still, the Preakness is more than just a horse race - it's an event. Every year, the city throws a huge "party," simply called "Preakness Week." Events including hot air balloon races, concerts and gala parties culminate with the actual race on a Saturday afternoon. Spectators fill the grandstands and pack the infield at Pimlico Race Course as the nation's finest thoroughbreds swiftly gallop around the track, adorned in the bright colors of their stables.

Horse racing continues year round at several race tracks around the city. Many of the nation's most renowned thoroughbreds hail from Maryland farms too, where owners and jockeys alike dream of capturing the horseshoe shaped crown of black-eyed susans that adorn the champions of Preakness races.

Many other equestrian events also fill the Baltimore calendar. Polo is an increasingly popular sport, and it is played at several locations in the Baltimore suburbs. Jousting, the ancient state sport in which riders spear a small ring sus-pended from posts, is still watched at fairs and festivals too, as are fox hunts and other races like the Hunt Cup.

And of course, one must always remember the boating activities available at the harbor and on the bay. Marinas dot the coast of the bay from Ocean City to Baltimore, as thousands of Baltimoreans man power yachts and sailboats on cool summer weekends.

All over town, people are talking about sports. Catch a fan with that magic glow in their eye, and they'll be glad to sit down with a tall cool drink and talk about their favorite pastime, whether its the Colts, a new sailboat, or an Oriole winning streak. Or go out to the "Yard" for yourself and check out a ball game. You're certainly welcome there. A word of advise, though. Try to brush up on your trivia. And be prepared to make a little noise.

The Baltimore Orioles have been one of the most successful sports franchises in history since they moved
to the city from St. Louis in 1954. Winners of half-a-dozen pennants and three World Series,
the hometown club has sent several players to the Hall of Fame recently, including
Brooks and Frank Robinson and Jim Palmer. On the field at Oriole Park, the team exudes a special spirit
labeled "Oriole Magic" which the city shares with record crowds and boisterous enthusiasm.

"If you build it, they will come," was a popular refrain around town while the Orioles new stadium was being constructed. And the fans have come, day and night, for great baseball at Camden Yards. With a breathtaking view of the city's skyline past the center field bleachers, its massive brick warehouse in right field, and old-fashioned detailing all over the park, the ballpark is a temple of delights for the serious baseball fan. Players, too, have rejoiced in the wonderful blend of old and new that Camden Yards offers fans on, and off, the field.

Ball players and columnists all around the country have always acknowledged that Baltimore has avid, knowledgable fans. The love affair between the city and the team runs deep, and it shows. Whether its an autograph seeker with his favorite "Bird" before the game, or a packed house rooting for the home team, there's an intimate relationship between the players and the fans that is unmatched in other Major League cities. The Orioles also play a crucial role in the community, offering assistance to a wide array of organizations and groups, including literacy programs, youth assistance and hospitals.

Part of what makes Oriole Park so unique is its attention to details. A row of shops and eateries line the
sidewalk along the Camden Yards warehouse that stretches out past the right field seats, and interesting
murals and old-fashioned signs crop up in practically every nook and cranny.
The Camden Yards Station rises majestically at the northeast end of the stadium, its red-brick fascade
and white Victorian copulas reminding visitors and fans of the mix of old and new that makes
"The Yard" a truly unique place to "catch the baseball fever."

Ice Hockey has always been a popular sport in Baltimore. The Baltimore Arena has played host to several hockey teams representing the city: first the Clippers and then the Skipjacks. Although the team here is not a member of the National Hockey League, the sport's "major leagues," the fast paced game has always attracted enthusiastic crowds, and the competition is never less than first rate.

The Baltimore Arena is also the host to many other major sporting events. Most recently, the U.S. Olympic Gymnastic Trials were held here. The final competitions for determining the U.S. Olympic gymnastics team, the week long event attracted huge crowds downtown to witness men's and women's events that were filled with atheleticism, grace and lots of drama. The city greeted these events with pomp and ceremony, reminding the entire world that Baltimore is a "major league" sports town.

Pimlico

Point-to-Point

Pimlico

Jousting

Race horse breeding and equestrian sports are often closely linked with Maryland history itself. Racing at several tracks around town, including the Pimlico Race Track, has become part of Baltimore's sports history that dates back to the beginning of the 19th century. The Preakness, the second leg of racing's prestigious Triple Crown, takes place at Pimlico every May. Jousting, Maryland's state sport, is an ancient equestrian event that still draws crowds at fairs and summer gatherings throughout the state.

In the countryside around Baltimore, fox hunts still bring out Baltimore's horse enthusiasts for spring and summer get-togethers. Wide open farmlands with pockets of wooded areas are the perfect spots for this time-honored English sport. Many clubs and equestrian centers around the state organize fox hunts, and large crowds still venture out to the countryside, picnic baskets full, for the thrill of the chase.

Baltimore, like any other great city, has its share of fine colleges and universities. Johns Hopkins University,
internationally acclaimed, is probably the city's most famous center of learning and research.
Located on the spacious Homewood campus, and named after federal style mansion, the Homewood
House at its center, Hopkins is probably best known for its medical education and research,
its liberal arts department and its writing program. The Hopkins M.F.A. program in writing attracts some
of the world's most famous authors to the campus.

COLLEGES AND UNIVERSITIES

Baltimore has often been perceived as strictly a working-class town. Yet among Baltimore's institutions of higher learning are one of the country's first medical schools, a nationally recognized music conservatory, and one of the most respected centers of medical research in the world.

Beginning in 1807, with the founding of the University of Maryland, the city has been a regional educational focal point. The history of the University is a litany of educational firsts. The medical school was the first to build a hospital for clinical instruction. A century and a half later, the establishment of the Shock Trauma Unit pioneered research in the treatment of accident-related trauma. Other leading research and patient care specialties at the University include the Intensive Care Neo-Natal Center, the Baltimore Cancer Research Program, and the National Institute for Sudden Infant Death Syndrome.

Today's University of Maryland at Baltimore (the home campus is now in College Park, about thirty miles southwest of Baltimore) also prepares students for careers in law, social work, nursing and dentistry. The dental school, when it opened in 1840, was the first institutional center of dental education in the world.

The University's second largest campus, University of Maryland Baltimore County, is outside the city in the western suburbs. With nearly 9,300 students, the Baltimore County Campus is a leader in Arts and Sciences education. It's theater department is especially noteworthy, and the library boasts a growing collection of local photography.

Philanthropists have played a major role in the development of higher education in Baltimore. Johns Hopkins grew up on a large farm in Anne Arundel County. He moved to Baltimore in 1813 to work for his uncle Gerard, a commission merchant and grocery distributor, and later made a fortune bottling whiskey. Investments in the port and the B&O Railroad made Hopkins one of the wealthiest men in the country. His will left eight million dollars for the establishment of the university and the hospital that bears his name.

Shortly after the turn of the century, Johns Hopkins University moved from downtown Baltimore to the Homewood campus, north of town. The site had descended from the family of Charles Carroll of Carrollton, and the magnificent Georgian home on the hillside, Homewood, belonged to one of Carroll's children. The modern campus, a blend of conservative classical buildings and contemporary structures, is a fitting home for Baltimore's internationally-known university. Today Johns Hopkins Hospital is a world-recognized medical training and research center.

George Peabody, whose million-dollar gift in 1859 established the Peabody Institute, was a native of Massachusetts. Like his compatriots, he earned a substantial fortune in Baltimore's mercantile exchanges and investment banks. His gift provided for "a library, a course of lectures, an academy of music, a gallery of art, and prizes to encourage private and public school pupils."

Peabody Institute eventually became the center of music in Baltimore. The core of the modern program is, of course, classical studies, and there is an impressive library. Also, the Peabody Jazz and Ragtime Ensembles have been known to make generations of Baltimoreans tap their toes. Its department of electronic music was among the first in the country to turn serious attention to what is now known as computer music.

The name Goucher is prominent in the history of education in Baltimore. Goucher College, now in Towson north of Baltimore, was incorporated in 1885 as the Women's College of Baltimore. The first president, Dr. John Goucher, donated the site for the main building on North Charles Street.

Dr. Goucher had already given land and an endowment to the Methodist Conferences of Baltimore for the buildings of the Centenary Bible Institute, now Morgan State University. In 1890 the school began to confer general degrees and the name changed to Morgan College, named for an early member of the Board of Trustees and important donor. Morgan's department of urban planning is recognized as a leader in the field and the school has long been a bastion of black cultural arts.

Another school established to train Baltimore's black youth opened its doors in 1900 as the Colored Training School, with a curriculum dedicated to training teachers. It was renamed the Fannie Jackson Coppin Normal School, after a former slave who was the first black woman in America to earn a college degree. Today's Coppin State College offers a full undergraduate liberal arts curriculum from its west Baltimore campus.

Many Baltimore colleges have religious sponsorship. In 1848 the Sisters of Notre Dame established a boarding school, and in 1873 the land for the college's Charles Street campus was purchased. By 1899 Notre Dame was conferring college-level degrees, and does so still. Neighboring Loyola College began instruction in 1852 with a faculty of eight Jesuits, conducting classes from two houses on Holliday Street. Loyola now offers both undergraduate and graduate curriculums and has been a leader in business education in Baltimore. Countless local executives boast a Loyola MBA on their resumes.

Two-year schools complement the efforts of these colleges.

The Community College of Baltimore is one of the first of its kind. CCB has, since its inception in 1947, offered courses that are directed specifically to the needs of the community. Its Center for English as a Second Language was established to help foreign students, and the Liberty Campus Child Development Center addresses the needs of urban pre-school education.

The University of Baltimore, created as a four-year college and eventually becoming a leading local law school, now offers only junior and senior level classes at its Mount Royal Avenue campus. The popularity of community colleges, all of which confer a two-year Associate of Arts degree, made it apparent that a school which would meet the needs of the community college students was needed.

Towson State University has its roots in Baltimore and has since developed into one of the largest campuses in the Baltimore area. Eleven students enrolled in what was originally strictly a teachers' college, the Maryland State Normal School, when it first operated from North Paca Street in 1869. By 1915 the campus had settled at its permanent location in what was rural Towson. Today it is Towson State University, and though many of its 15,000 students are destined to teach, the university offers a full range of liberal arts curriculums.

One of Baltimore's strengths has always been, and continues to be, the quality of its educational resources. This fact does not go unnoticed in the business community, where new technology companies take advantage of the work done at research centers like the Space Telescope Science Institute at JHU or the University of Maryland Foundation's Research Park, now under development. The park will facilitate interaction between the university's faculty, its research efforts, and the business community.

The contributions of the city's educational institutions have always exceeded what could be expected from a city of Baltimore's size. The dedication of the city's educators, coupled with the efforts of government and business, will assure Baltimore a prominent place in education and research for years to come.

Johns Hopkins University, a privately endowed college, was founded in 1876. Since the time of its first president, Daniel Coit Gilman, the university has been a world-renowned center for education and research. Its stately brick halls and buildings outline a tree-lined square that makes up its popular studying and meeting place, known as the quad. Shriver Hall occupies one end of the university's beautiful sylvan quad. It is here that many of the finest minds of the nation lecture, and where bands and entertainers perform for students and residents of the city alike.

Located on Charles Street, in the heart of Charles Village, the Johns Hopkins University offers many wide-open spaces for study, rest and relaxation. Spacious green lawns and tree-lined walks remind students of the classical education that Hopkins epitomizes. Whether its casual recreation, small-talk among students, or solitary contemplation, the campus offers beautiful spaces in which to accomplish any kind of thought or interaction.

Spine Surgery Johns Hopkins Hospital

Brain Surgery Johns Hopkins Hospital

Main Building - Johns Hopkins Hospital

The Johns Hopkins Hospital opened in 1889, on a site selected by Hopkins himself. With the Johns Hopkins School of Medicine following four years later, the two revolutionized the training of physicians and the nature of medical research, thus becoming one of the most respected hospitals in the world. Recently, when first lady Hilary Clinton presented a major speech on the status of American health care, she choose Hopkins as the site for the speech because of its symbolic preeminence as one of the worlds greatest medical institutions.

Main Building - Johns Hopkins Hospital

Located in the rotunda of the main building at Johns Hopkins Hospital,
the Christ Statue has become a popular attraction at the institution. Greeting all visitors and patients
who enter the hospital, the statue's features are worn smooth in areas from people who rub it
while praying for good news and good health.

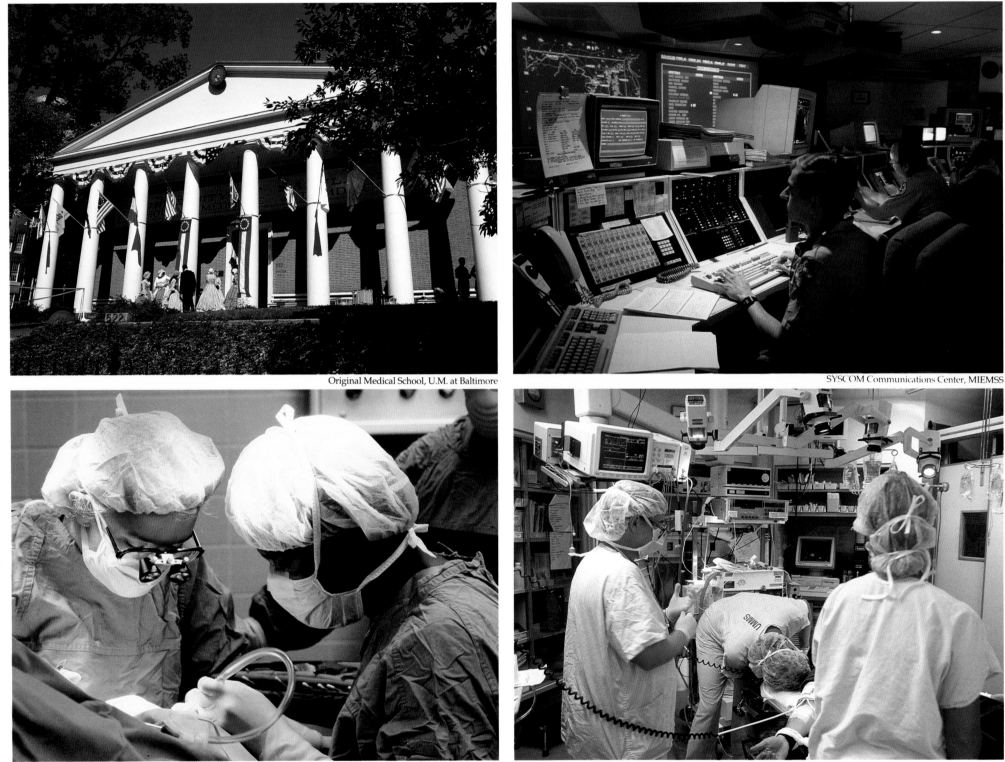

Original Medical School, U.M. at Baltimore

SYSCOM Communications Center, MIEMSS

Operation, U.M. at Baltimore

Emergency Treatment Shock Trauma Center

Founded in 1807, the University of Maryland at Baltimore is one of the oldest medical schools in the nation. The School of Law was formed in 1812, and was the first to provide a clearly defined educational framework for law students. The Dental School (1840), and the Schools of Pharmacy (1841) and Nursing (1889) were added later, making the university a leader in patient care education. Today, UMAB is a leader in research, patient care and high-tech medical training. It is most noted for its Shock Trauma Center and its work in the fields of neonatal care and Sudden Infant Death Syndrome.

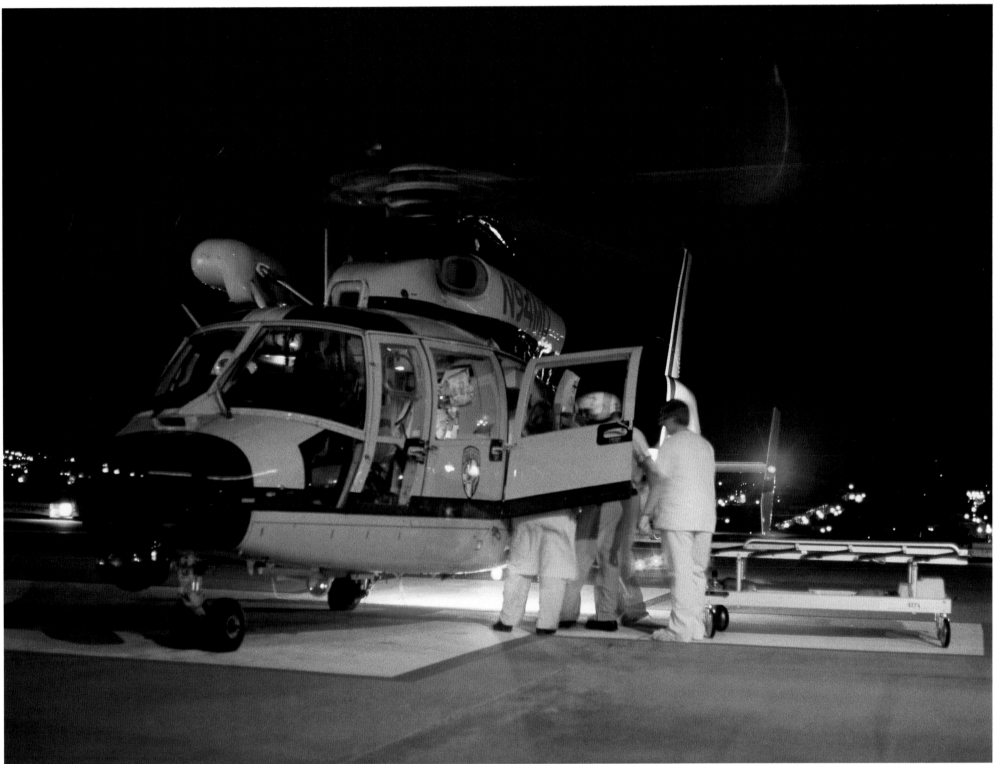

State Police Helicopter with patient for Shock Trauma Center

The R Adams Cowley Shock Trauma Center at the University of Maryland Medical Center
is internationally known for its excellence in emergency medical care. Located at the
University of Maryland Hospital, the Trauma Center was the brainchild of Dr. R Adams Cowley.
Accepting work that is constantly demanding, the staff routinely rushes against the clock
to provide life-saving care to critically injured accident victims. The center is also a pioneer
in the development of high-tech care for trauma victims.

Towson State University

Towson State University

Goucher College

Ever-expanding since it acquired university status in 1976, Towson State University currently offers a growing variety of undergraduate and graduate degrees. Its facilities include fine theatres and art galleries, just to name a few. Goucher College moved from cramped city quarters to the wide open spaces of Towson in 1953. A women's college until just recently, the school was named after Dr. John Goucher, a prominent Baltimore educator from the late 19th century.

Loyola College

The University Of Baltimore

Morgan State University

Founded by Father John Early in 1852, Loyola College has occupied a lush wooded area along
Charles Street since 1922. Loyola is particularly noted for its excellence in liberal arts and
business administration. The University of Baltimore was founded in 1925, and prepares students for
careers in government and business. It is also particularly well-known for its law school.
Morgan State University is nationally acclaimed for extending educational opportunities to African-
American students. Founded as the Centenary Bible Institute, it offers a full range of degrees, and is located
on one of Baltimore's most beautiful campuses.

125

Nearly ten years in the making, the Seagirt Marine Terminal has projected the port of Baltimore into the twenty-first century. The huge, blue twenty-story cranes seem to scrape the sky as they effortlessly unload container cargo ships at record speeds. Opened in late 1989, the $220 million, state-of-the-art terminal can accommodate the largest container ships from around the world. The project, run by the Maryland Port Administration, has provided hundreds of jobs for Marylanders, and promises to keep the port on the cutting edge of the marine shipping industry for decades to come.

THE PORT

When the first settlers in Baltimore set up shop along the banks of the Patapsco in the early 1700's, it was the potential port which drew them to the spot. They recognized its easy access to the Chesapeake Bay, its vast protective harbor, the prosperity of nearby agricultural sectors in neighboring colonies, and its proximity to the already-flourishing waterfront villages of Fells Point and Jonestown.

What they could not have imagined was the role the Port of Baltimore would play in international affairs in coming centuries, largely due to attributes of the port they could not have foreseen. As the American hinterland developed, it happened that Baltimore was the harbor closest to the burgeoning West by virtue of its inland location. As manufacturing centers like Pittsburgh emerged from the mountainous wilderness, the benefits of shipping into and out of Baltimore were magnified.

This prime location was the impetus for the early development of the American railroad system, with Baltimore as its heart and soul. Trains strengthened the link between the Maryland city and the factories westward, and the Port of Baltimore became a railroad port.

By 1812, *Niles Weekly Register* could report that the city had attained "a degree of commercial importance which has brought down upon it the envy and jealousy of all the great cities in the Union." The War of 1812 boosted shipbuilding and sent Baltimore Clippers to ports throughout the western world. The resources developed meshed nicely with the railroad, which began to dominate the port by the Civil War. While that war devastated trade in general, Baltimore emerged stronger than ever, expanding its trade as the rails crisscrossed the country.

Small Chesapeake Bay boats called here, filled with produce from the Eastern Shore in the summer and oysters in the fall and winter. Larger schooners, huge vessels carrying as many as five tall masts, ferried lumber from Baltimore to South America and the West Indies, returning with copra or dyes destined for the aniline works along Boston Street.

Baltimore`s access to growing points inland was secured by the railroad, canals, and other modes of transportation. The first major dredging of the channel came in 1892, allowing several new terminals to be built just after the turn of the century. By 1920, Baltimore was a port of call for thirty-nine overseas steamship lines, thirteen coastal companies, and nine intercoastal shipping lines.

Passenger travel was also a large part of the life of the port until just after World War II. The Old Bay Line steamers, among others, served all parts of the Chesapeake region, and many Baltimoreans looked forward to a leisurely cruise from Baltimore to Richmond, Norfolk, or north to Head of Elk with connections to Philadelphia. The era closed with several boats operating from the harbor near today`s Harborplace to resorts on the Eastern Shore like Tolchester and Betterton.

With the demise of the paddlewheeler came other changes that would threaten Baltimore's dominance of Middle Atlantic shipping. In the early 1970's the port was still handling record volumes of cargo, dependent on four commodities: oil, grain, coal, and iron ore. Ships from Baltimore were bound to ports like Calcutta and Sao Paulo. These third world labor forces had begun to compete with traditional Baltimore industries like shoemaking and clothing manufacturing, and soon the city was importing consumer goods from these points as well as Taiwan, Hong Kong, and other Far East centers of newly-emerging economic strength.

Shipbuilding was still an important port activity through the early post-war years. The first container ships were built here in 1954 and the first jumbo oil tankers shortly thereafter. Freighters increased in size tenfold in just a decade, necessitating a deepening of the channel as well as adjustment of all land-based port facilities. Cranes were installed at the Dundalk Marine Terminal to handle the new container tonnage. A mechanized iron ore pier was built in Sparrows Point and a jungle of cement silos grew in Curtis Bay to accommodate the massive maws of the new ships.

But at the same time the port found itself still shackled to the railroad interests that owned much of the commercial waterfront, particularly within the Baltimore city limits. The railroad industry was moribund and capital-poor, paying little in taxes while controlling the most valuable industrial development land in Baltimore.

It was clear as early as 1950 that a controlling authority would have to be established to coordinate the needed development. In 1956 the Maryland Port Authority was created, and in 1971 it became the Maryland Port Administration.

Today's port serves the trading needs of a number of partners, notably in Europe and Asia. The port's two largest import trade partners are Japan and West Germany. The major trading partner in terms of tonnage is nearby Canada. The export trade, both measured in dollars and tons, is smaller than the imports, and once again Japan and West Germany are the two main partners.

Coal and grain are still the leading commodities to pass through the port on the export side. Food products make up about a tenth of the exported material that passes down the Chesapeake from Baltimore's waterfront. On the import side, raw materials such as lumber, minerals and rubber still dominate trade in Baltimore, though automobiles have become an important new source of import tonnage.

Through the combined efforts of private trading companies and the Maryland Port Administration, the competitive advantages of the Port of Baltimore are marketed on an international basis. As a result, new markets are opening and merchandise is arriving at a growing rate from South America and Europe. Deeper access channels are being dredged to accommodate modern ships, and improvements in existing facilities will assure that the port enters the twenty-first century with adequate incentives to attract cargo.

The slogan of the Maryland Port Administration is "We Make It Work," a promise that is based on the port's dedication to providing the best service on the East Coast. That devotion to continuing the port's tradition of success, coupled with a zealous drive to modernization, will keep Baltimore among the world's leaders in international trade.

Some of the world's largest freighters and container ships travel into the harbor to be loaded and unloaded at the Dundalk and Seagirt Marine Terminals. From its beginnings, Baltimore has been one of the nation's major ports, due largely to the city's ideal location and its sophisticated railway systems. Since the mid-1950's, with the creation of the Maryland Port Authority (currently the Maryland Port Administration), the state has coordinated efforts to remain on the industry's cutting edge with marine facility developments that are capable of handling cargo from all markets of the world.

The final berth of the Dundalk Marine Terminal was completed in 1982, allowing the port to accommodate all types of cargo and container ships. During the last several decades, the terminal, along with the efforts of the Maryland Port Administration, has allowed Baltimore to remain at the forefront of the shipping industry. Although it ships and receives all types of cargo, the Dundalk Marine Terminal is most famous for the tens of thousands of cars that it imports yearly.

Everyone agrees that the Seagirt Marine Terminal is the most efficient marine terminal in the world. What makes the entire project work, though, are its people. The result of the entire community - the state, labor, and the private sector - the $220-million terminal is only as good as the crane operators, cargo handlers, drivers and clerks who work there. The terminal promises to provide hundreds of jobs to the state, and hopes to remain at the forefront of the shipping industry for years to come.

The Seagirt Marine Terminal is a monument to the latest in maritime technology. Located just south of the Inner Harbor, Seagirt's 265-acre terminal offers three deepwater berths that can handle the world's largest vessels. A 70-acre railyard, fourteen inbound and five outbound truck lanes, and nearby access to major highways, insures that cargo can be unloaded and on its way to destinations all over the country in the quickest possible time. With its high efficiency cranes, Seagirt has delivered on its promise to be one of the most productive shipping terminals in the world.

131

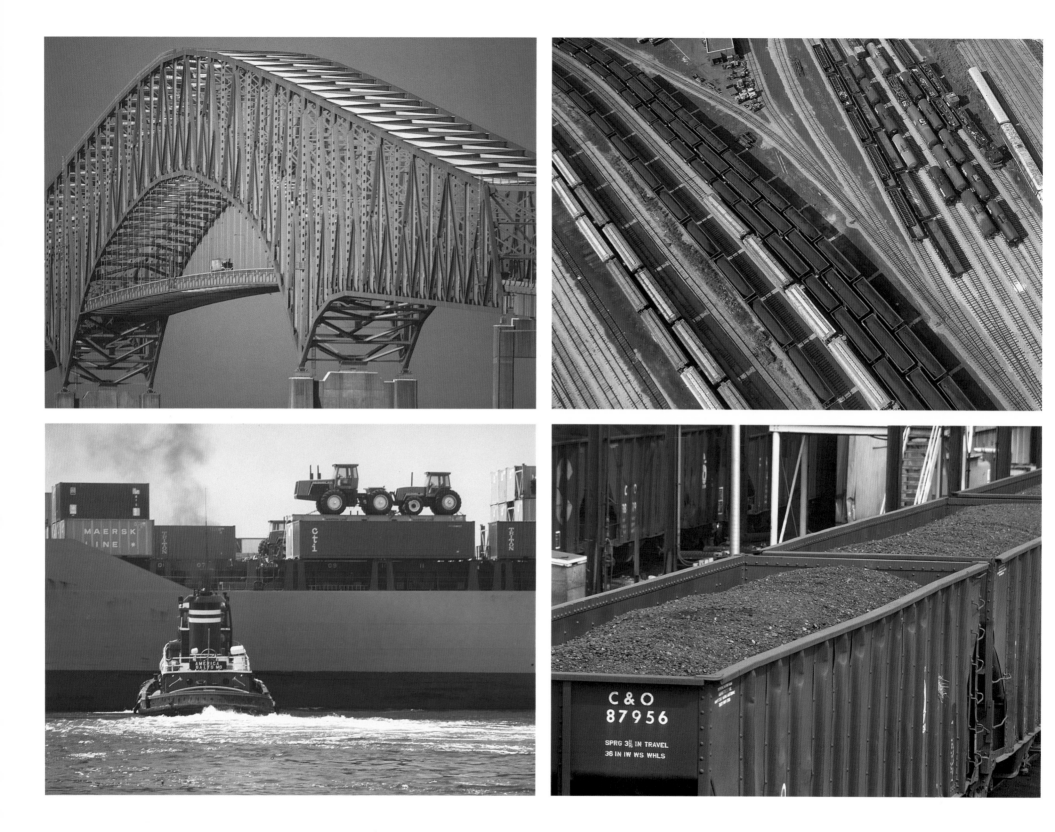

The old axiom that a business's success depends on its location certainly pertains to the port of Baltimore. Centrally located up the calm, protected waters of the Chesapeake Bay, Baltimore has been one of the nation's major ports since the city's infancy. And because of its long history, the state has been able to develop a complex system of roads and railways to support the port's strengths. To or from the shipyards, cargo can be sent anywhere in the world quickly and efficiently because of the city's location and infrastructure.

Two newcomers in Baltimore's quest for better mass transit are the subway and light rail systems. Reaching from the city to northwest Baltimore County, the subway allows quick and inexpensive access for commuters heading in or out of Baltimore. The light rail system, with its first leg completed in the spring of 1992, stretches from Camden Yards to central Baltimore County. A model for many other mass transit systems in the nation, Baltimore's light rail is fast and environmentally friendly. Plans for its expansion include access to South Baltimore and Northern Baltimore County.

The ultra-modern design of Baltimore-Washington International Airport practically beckons adventurous globe-trotters to explore far-away lands. Easily accessed and just minutes south of the city, BWI has increased its services to include a multitude of domestic and international airlines and routes, as well as offering an efficient air freight business. Despite its size, the design of the airport gives travelers stress-free access, whether they are entering or leaving the city.

Many Baltimoreans still fondly recall the days when the Baltimore-Washington International Airport
was called "Friendship." Although it offers a growing list of services, and a more complex system of routes,
the airport still seems more spacious and manageable than its neighbors in Washington, D.C.
The airport, both as Friendship and BWI, has a long history of greeting heroes and sports champions home
to Baltimore after victories in events such as the Super Bowl, the World Series and the Olympics.

Ellicott Machine Corporation International is the world's leading producer of cutter suction dredges. Since 1885 innovative engineering and high standards of quality have kept Ellicott in the forefront of dredge manufactures. Ellicott's dredges were used to build the Panama Canal. Ellicott has in fact designed and built over 1,200 dredges, more than any other manufacturer, and has served customers in over 65 countries. The only builder in the world which designs and manufactures all key components of the dredging system. Because of this single responsibility approach, many of Ellicott's dredges are still going strong after 50 years of service.

The only sizeable oil company headquartered in Maryland, Crown Central Petroleum Corporation is a long established refiner and distributor of petroleum products throughout the state as well as the Mid-Atlantic and Southeastern regions. The company's clean and efficient retail outlets, coupled with its wholesale operations, are supplied by two refineries which are located in Houston and Tyler, Texas. Product is distributed along the Colonial and Plantation Pipelines at 16 proprietary terminals. With gross sales of $2 billion, this Fortune 500 corporation is one of the largest companies headquartered in Baltimore. Crown is a long-time supporter of community activities in the city and the state.

A home is where the American dream comes to life. Making that dream become a reality is **Ryland**'s business. Since its founding in 1967 in Columbia, Maryland, Ryland has grown to become one of the nation's leading homebuilding and mortgage-services companies. Today, Ryland is building on its strong reputation by making dreams come true in more that forty U. S. markets, as well as internationally.

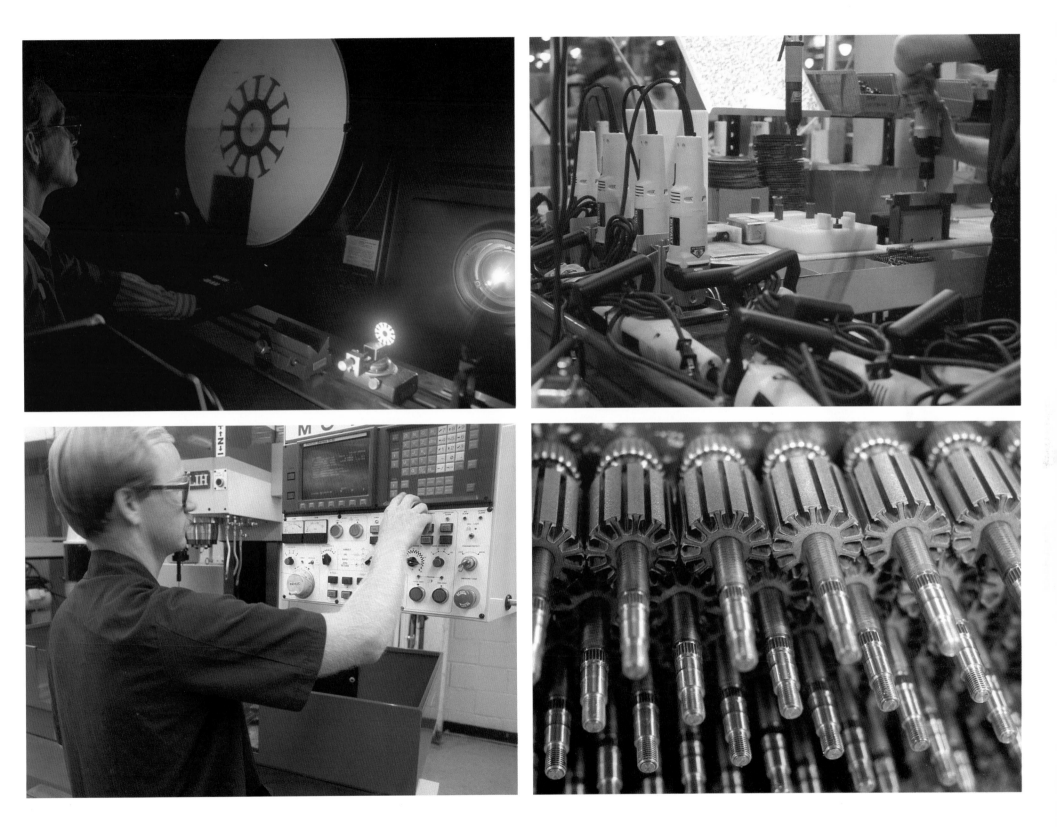

With products and services marketed in over 100 countries, Black & Decker is a global marketer and
manufacturer of quality products used in and around the home and for commercial applications.
The company enjoys global brand name recognition, and its product lines hold top market share positions
in their respective industries. Black & Decker is the world's largest producer of power tools, power tool
accessories, and security hardware (Kwikset); its household products business is the
North American leader in the small appliance industry; and it is the fastest growing
major faucet manufacturer (Price Pfister) in the United States.

143

On August 15,1943 **H&S Bakery** opened its doors for business. Its founders, Harry Tsakalos and Steve Paterakis, with Steve's son John made bread by hand and baked in a hearth baked oven. From this modest beginning in a basement the bakery has grown into a 210,000 square foot complex. Harry and John foresaw the rapid growing fast food industry in the early 60's; Athens Automatic Rolls, a state-of-the-art roll plant, produced 3,000 dozen hamburger buns an hour when opened in 1965.

This venture eventually grew into Northeast Foods, Inc. which is still owned by the Paterakis and the Tsakalos families. There are currently 9 divisions operating in 7 states with distribution into 23 states. The bakeries are now producing 370,000 rolls an hour, nearly 2 billion rolls a year! The companies also serve and supply private label bread and rolls to supermarkets and other wholesale bakeries and distributors. Harry and Liberty Tsakalos and son Nick, and John Paterakis and sons Steve, Bill, John Jr. and Chuck are all involved in the management and operation of H&S Bakery and its affiliates. Today there are more than 2,000 employees system-wide and the fleet includes 120 delivery vans and 200 tractor trailers.

The Greater Baltimore Committee

Executive Plazas in Hunt Valley

O'Conor, Piper, & Flynn

The Galleria and Atrium

The Greater Baltimore Committee is Baltimore's only regional economic development organization that takes a strategic, problem-solving approach to meeting the economic challenges of this region.

O'Conor, Piper & Flynn Realtors was founded in 1984 by the merger of 5 Maryland-based real estate companies. Since that time it has grown to 38 offices located throughout Maryland and Southern Pennsylvania, with almost 1,500 sales associates. Award winning office and retail complexes that radiate the "corporate" in "corporate image" is what is projected in the properties which are owned and operated by **Hill Management Services, Inc.** The Galleria Towers and the Atrium, and The Executive Plazas in Hunt Valley are examples of their properties.

The General Motors Truck and Bus Group Assembly Plant in Baltimore, originally built and
in continuous operation since 1935, is the only plant which builds the popular M-Van for Chevrolet
and GMC. Due to a $300 million modernization program began in 1984 the plant is a showcase of
high technology. It has the world's first "modular paint system" using 98 robots which are also used
throughout the plant in other stages of vehicle assembly. Employing about 4,000 people,
the plant has an economic impact of over $300 million in the Baltimore economy
between its payroll and purchases from local suppliers.

BethShip Drydock

BethShip Graving Dock

BethShip Drydock

BethShip Graving Dock

BethShip Sparrows Point Yard is a full service repair and conversion shipyard conveniently located near Baltimore, with access from either Chesapeake or Delaware Bays. The yard's modern facilities include: a graving dock measuring 365 m by 61 m for vessels up to 300,000 dwt; a floating drydock with lifting capacity of 40,000 tons, nearly 1,000 m of berthing space; and a complete line of full service shops.
In addition to voyage repair and overhaul work, BethShip has the expertise and the facilities for complex conversions and life extension programs. BethShip also has a long and proud history of ship construction. Since shipbuilding began at Sparrows Point in 1891, more than 600 new ships have sailed from the yard. Above all BethShip is committed to quality. From workmanship and material control to planning, scheduling and delivery, BethShip's quality and performance record is unsurpassed.

Grace Davison, a business unit of W. R. Grace & Co., has been a part of Baltimore since its founding in 1832 by William T. Davison. Originally "An acidulator of old bones and fossils", or fertilizer manufacturer, Grace Davison has grown over the last 160 years to become one of the world's premier producers of specialty inorganic chemicals. Grace Davison's Curtis Bay Works, located in southwest Baltimore, is the largest of the company's six worldwide manufacturing facilities. Construction of the plant was started in 1888; new construction and renovations on current operations are continuous. The Works produces silica gel for use in paints, edible oils, food, pharmaceuticals, insulated glass and dehydrating agents; fluid cracking catalysts for converting crude oil into gasoline; and polyolefin catalysts, which are used in the production of plastics.

BG&E's Natural Gas Vehicle and Electric programs promote clean alternative fuels that foster a healthier environment for our future generations.

BG&E's prototype Smart House uses microprocessor technology to provide state-of-the art communications, control and energy distribution systems designed to offer the homeowner a safer and energy efficient residence.

Maryland has often been called "America in Miniature," and the phrase rings true when visiting
Baltimore's surrounding areas. From the Appalacian mountains to the west, the rolling,
wooded farmlands of Central Maryland, to the wide sandy beaches at Ocean City, Maryland certainly
offers all types of terrain and the lifestyles that are associated with them. Because of its much noted
Chesapeake Bay, the Baltimore region offers great sailing, a plethora of water activites,
and of course, spectacular seafood, all within a few hours drive of the city.

SURROUNDING AREAS

Baltimore attorney Peter Carnes constructed a 35-foot balloon out of "beautiful, costly and variegated silks" in the spring of 1784. On June 3, Carnes ascended above Baltimore from Howard Woods, the site of today's Washington Monument. The event was unofficially the first balloon ascension in the United States.

If Carnes had recorded what he saw from above the city he would have written that all roads led to Baltimore. Along Rolling Road he would have seen plantation workers rolling hogsheads of tobacco from Baltimore County to the wharves along the Patapsco. From Ellicott's Mills in Howard County he would have reported wagons of grain slowly moving along Frederick Road into the city. He could not have missed traffic along Philadelphia Road nor could he have ignored the sailing vessels making their way to the harbors of Fells Point and Baltimore Town.

Two hundred years later a similar event takes place annually: the Preakness Balloon Race. The balloon captains could draw much the same conclusion as Carnes. Trucks approach Baltimore from every direction filled with all manner of goods. Ships lie in the harbor waiting to discharge cargo from around the world and fill their holds with ore, cement, or coal. Baltimore has become permanently established as the focal point of the entire region.

To be the economic and cultural heart of a state as diverse as Maryland is quite an accomplishment. More than anything, it is the Chesapeake Bay that defines what Baltimore is and why it has developed as it has. This wide, salty estuary has for generations provided a bountiful harvest for the tables of Baltimoreans and others, and its deep shipping lanes have carried both goods and people into the city.

The state capital in Annapolis is one of the best-preserved colonial cities in America, keeping not only its eighteenth century appearance, but also its southern tradition of hospitality. For nearly three hundred years the state legislature has met here annually in the State House, with its commanding view of the city and the small harbor. Maryland's elected representatives still meet in the same building that hosted Washington, Madison, Jefferson and their contemporaries. The streets of Annapolis are lined with ancient homes; many carefully restored residences, and others converted to shops and restaurants.

At Solomon's Island, in southern Maryland's Calvert County, the Chesapeake Bay is about nine miles wide. Just across the choppy water is the Eastern Shore (the only region in Maryland whose name, by agreement among residents, should be capitalized). The Bay is more than just a geographic division. As far as Eastern Shore citizens are concerned, it delineates an area which is culturally and socially distinct.

It's hard to deny that they have a point, for almost immediately after crossing the Chesapeake Bay Bridge near Annapolis the feeling of a slower-paced, tradition-bound society descends. Little seems to have changed here, largely because Eastern Shore people have never been in a hurry to adopt "progress." Watermen bristle at the thought of state control over the Chesapeake and its Eastern Shore tributaries, defending their age-old right to freely harvest the Bay's bounty.

To many it appears that the region's single concession to the twentieth century is Ocean City, the state's only Atlantic resort, stretching along miles of sandy beach. "OC" is the destination of tens of thousands of vacationers who head east every weekend from May through September. There's a superb beach, excellent hotels, restaurants and night spots. Nearby Assateague Island is popular among campers, fishermen, amateur naturalists and beach bums.

The middle and upper shores have managed to pass through three centuries virtually unscathed. Easton, the unofficial capital of the area, has kept its small-town personality. Its streets are lined with shops whose windows display Eastern Shore fashion (hunting and sailing garb), carved decoys and waterfowl art.

It is the western shore, particularly the state's broad, fertile central section that extends from the Bay to Pennsylvania to the north and to the foothills of the Appalachians in the west, that is Maryland's economic pulse. Baltimore, of course, provides the infrastructure - the financial institutions, the port, and much of the work force - upon which central Maryland depends. Major industrial parks have sprung up from former farmlands around the Baltimore Beltway. Cattle still graze within sight of a rapidly-growing high technology center near Gaithersburg. The proximity of the nation's capital has attracted all manner of enterprise to the Maryland counties which border Washington, D.C.

To the west, as one enters Frederick County, the Appalachian Mountains begin to rear above the farms. Frederick, a nineteenth century railroad town that is popular for its century-old buildings and its small-town personality, is the gateway to the Maryland mountain playground. Beyond the county's rocky fields the entire character of the state changes. Centuries after the first settlers made their way through the mountain passes to settle in towns like Cumberland and Hagerstown, there's still a pioneering feeling here. Western Marylanders acknowledge the existence of Baltimore, and some will even admit the economic importance of the distant city, but still defend their independence from Baltimore in particular and city-life in general.

Garrett County is as far as one can go from Baltimore and still be in Maryland, and maybe the influence of Baltimore this far west is eclipsed by much-closer Pittsburgh. Yet thousands of Marylanders make Garrett County's green spaces, mountains and lakes their vacation favorite. Perhaps more than any other resort spot in the state, the western Maryland mountains can claim to have year-round attractions, for they draw fishermen, campers, and sun-seekers in the summer and skiers after the weather turns cold.

For many years Maryland has touted itself as "America in Miniature." Baltimore is the focal point of the diverse state, its economic heart. But this is a two-way street. Without the resources of the lands surrounding the city, and without the easy access from Baltimore to points west, there would be no port on the Patapsco River. Though a waterman on Smith Island or a mountain family in Cresaptown may disagree, the partnership between Baltimore and Maryland has been healthy and mutually beneficial.

State House, Annapolis

Paca House, Annapolis

U.S.N.A., Annapolis

State House, Annapolis

Once the nation's capital, Annapolis has been Maryland's state capital since 1694. In fact, the State House is the oldest building in the nation to be used as a continuous seat of local government. The city also has more pre-Revolutionary brick buildings than any other city in the country, making it a must visit for buffs of American history. Today, Annapolis is the home of the U.S. Naval Academy, which was founded in 1845. It is also a growing tourist attraction, with great yachting, spectacular shopping and fine restaurants.

Point Lookout, Southern Maryland

Ocean City, Eastern Shore

Tobacco Farm, Southern Maryland

Ocean City, Eastern Shore

Southern Maryland and the Eastern Shore, with its low, flat farmlands, creates a completely different lifestyle from the hustle and bustle of Baltimore city. Historically noted for its fine tobacco farms and great water activities, these areas exude a slow-paced southern charm that still survives despite their proximity to Washington, D.C. and Baltimore. Ocean City, a narrow barrier island at the state's eastern border, is a favorite summer vacation attraction for residents all over the Pennsylvania-Maryland-Virginia area.

Ledew Topiary

The Capitol Building, Washington, D.C.

Deer Creek, Harford County

Jefferson Memorial, Washington, D.C.

Baltimore's surrounding areas are a study in contrast, with great wooded areas just miles from Washington, D.C., the nation's capital. Fresh water streams and rivers rush through dense wooded countryside throughout the state, particularly in Baltimore's surrounding counties. The Ladew Topiary Gardens are a favorite attraction in Harford County, one of Baltimore's growing suburbs. And just 40 miles down Route 95 is Washington, D.C., home of historic monuments, fine museums and national attractions like the Capitol, the Jefferson Memorial and the White House.

Muddy Bottom Falls, Western Maryland

Garrett County, Western Maryland

Garrett County, Western Maryland

Mist on Mountains, Western Maryland

West of Baltimore are more spectacular sites like rushing waterfalls, winding roads and breathtaking mountainous vistas. With a multitude of wooded parks and beautifully maintained campgrounds, the western Maryland region is a favorite for back-to-nature enthusiasts. In this area of the state, one can enjoy great hunting, fishing, or maybe just a calm walk on a nature trail beneath the shadows of tall trees. Western Maryland is a great weekend getaway from the daily pressures of city life.

Federal Hill at sunset or at sunrise, for the early risers, is one experience everyone in the city should enjoy at least once. On this particularly wondrous evening, all the lights in the city were on earlier than usual to celebrate Baltimore's hosting of the All-Star game. With blimps cruising overhead, the city was more exciting than ever.

MAPS – GUIDE

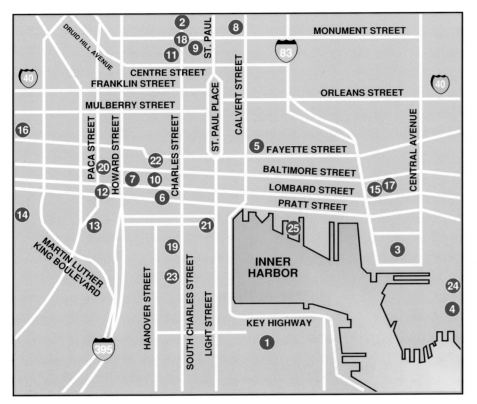

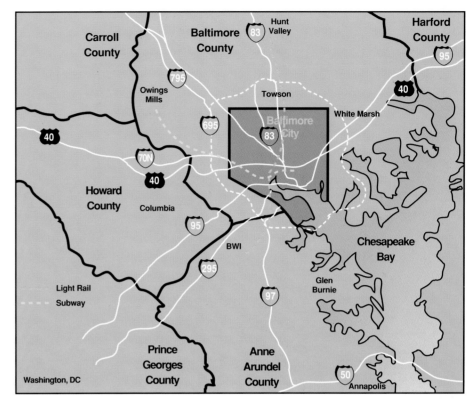

GENERAL AREAS
1. Federal Hill
2. Mount Vernon
3. Little Italy
4. Fells Point

GENERAL INTEREST
Mayor's Office ....(410) 396-3100
Chamber of Commerce ....(410) 296-0642
Baltimore Area Convention & Visitors Center ....(410) 837-4636
Mass Transit Administration ....(410) 539-5000
5. Baltimore City Hall ....(410) 396-4900
6. Baltimore Convention Center ....(410) 659-7000
Greater Baltimore Committee ....(410) 727-2820
7. Baltimore Arena ....(410) 347-2020
Baltimore Zoo ....(410) 366-5466
Lexington Market ....(410) 685-6169
Pimlico Race Course ....(410) 542-9400
Baltimore Washington Int'l Airport (BWI) ....(410) 859-7111

THE ARTS
Baltimore Center for the Performing Arts ....(410) 625-4200
Lyric Opera House ....(410) 685-0693
Baltimore Symphony Orchestra ....(410) 783-8000
8. Center Stage ....(410) 332-0033
9. Peabody Conservatory of Music ....(410) 659-8124
10. Morris A. Mechanic Theatre ....(410) 625-4230
Baltimore Museum of Art ....(410) 396-7101
11. The Walters Art Gallery ....(410) 547-9000
Maryland Institute, College of Art ....(410) 669-9200
12. Baltimore Arts Tower-Bromo Seltzer Tower ......(410) 396-4575

HISTORIC SITES
13. Babe Ruth Birthplace and Baseball Center ....(410) 727-1539
Baltimore Public Works Museum ....(410) 396-5565
Baltimore Maritime Museum ....(410) 396-3854
14. B&O Railroad Museum ....(410) 752-2490
The Cloisters Children's Museum ....(410) 823-2550
Great Blacks in Wax Museum ....(410) 563-3404
Jewish Historical Society of Maryland ....(410) 732-6400
Maryland Historical Society ....(410) 685-3750

15. Star-Spangled Banner Flag House & Museum ....(410) 837-1793
Baltimore Conservatory ....(410) 396-0180
16. Edgar Allan Poe House ....(410) 396-7932
Westminster Hall and E. A. Poe's Grave ....(410) 706-7228
Fort McHenry National Monument ....(410) 962-4290
Mount Clare Mansion ....(410) 837-3262
17. Shot Tower ....(410) 837-5424
Baltimore Museum of Industry ....(410) 727-4808
Baltimore Streetcar Museum ....(410) 547-0264
City Fire Museum ....(410) 727-2414
Carroll Mansion ....(410) 396-3524
H.L. Mencken House ....(410) 396-7997
Peale Museum ....(410) 396-1149
1840 House ....(410) 396-3279
Brewer's Park ....(410) 396-3523
Evergreen House ....(410) 516-0895
Mother Seton House ....(410) 523-3443
18. Washington Monument

INNER HARBOR
Water Taxi ....(800) 658-8947
Harborplace and The Gallery ....(410) 332-4191
Maryland Science Center ....(410) 685-5225
National Aquarium in Baltimore ....(410) 576-3800
Oriole Park at Camden Yards ....(410) 685-9500
Top of the World-World Trade Center ....(410) 837-4515
U.S. Frigate Constellation ....(410) 539-1797
Gilbane Properties, R.I. ....(401) 456-5890

SCHOOLS
Enoch Pratt Free Library ....(410) 396-5430
Johns Hopkins University ....(410) 516-8000
Johns Hopkins Hospital ....(410) 955-5000
University of Maryland at Baltimore ....(410) 706-3100
Towson State University ....(410) 830-2000
Goucher College ....(410) 337-6000
University of Baltimore ....(410) 837-4848
Loyola College ....(410) 617-2000
Morgan State University ....(410) 319-3333

LOCAL CORPORATIONS
Westinghouse ....(410) 765-1300
AT&T ....(800) 222-0400
Ellicott Machine ....(410) 837-7900

Crown Central Petroleum ....(410) 539-7400
General Motors Plant ....(410) 631-2000
Signet Bank ....(410) 332-5105
Ryland Homes, Inc. ....(410) 715-7000
Black & Decker ....(410) 716-3900
C&P Telephone ....(800) 539-9900
Baltimore Gas and Electric ....(410) 234-5000
W.R. Grace Company ....(410) 792-4868
O'Connor, Piper & Flynn ....(410) 561-8800
H & S Bakery – Northeast Foods ....(410) 276-7254
Pepsi Cola Company ....(410) 366-3500
Hill Management ....(410) 628-7000
Bethlehem Steel BethShip Yard ....(410) 388-7702

HOTELS-RESTAURANTS
Baltimore International Culinary College
Cooking Demonstration Theatre ....(410) 752-3279
19. Hyatt Regency ....(410) 528-1234
20. Marriott Inner Harbor ....(410) 962-0202
21. Sheraton Inner Harbor ....(410) 962-8300
22. Radisson Lord Baltimore ....(410) 539-8400
23. Harbor Court Hotel ....(410) 234-0550
24. Admiral Fell Inn ....(410) 522-2195
Stouffer Inner Harbor ....(410) 547-1200
Omni Inner Harbor ....(410) 752-1100
Sheraton Towson ....(410) 321-7400
Inn at Government House ....(410) 539-0566
Josef's ....(410) 877-7800
Peerce's Plantation ....(410) 252-3100
Da Mimmo ....(410) 727-6876
Velleggia's ....(410) 685-2620
Harrison's Pier 5 Clarion Inn ....(410) 783-5553
Central Station ....(410) 752-7133
Obrycki's Crab House ....(410) 732-6399
Tio Pepe ....(410) 539-4675
25. Chart House ....(410) 539-6616
Haussner's Restaurant ....(410) 327-8365
Days Inn-Timonium ....(410) 560-1000
Bohager's Bar and Grill ....(410) 563-7220
Hammerjacks ....(410) 752-3302
Milton Inn ....(410) 771-4366

As the sun sets over the Inner Harbor the "Spirit of Baltimore" almost symbolically surveys the glory
of the new Baltimore as it leaves on an evening cruise. The city's ever changing profile is a tribute
to those with vision, those who made the vision real, and those who enjoy its glory each and every day.